G000229291

ANGELS OF DEATH

ANGELS OF DEATH

Murderous Medics, Nefarious Nurses and Killer Carers

Al Cimino

This edition published in 2022 by Arcturus Publishing Limited
26/27 Bickels Yard, 151–153 Bermondsey Street,
London SE1 3HA

Copyright © Arcturus Holdings Limited

All rights reserved. No part of this publication may be reproduced,
stored in a retrieval system, or transmitted, in any form or by any means,
electronic, mechanical, photocopying, recording or otherwise, without
prior written permission in accordance with the provisions of the
Copyright Act 1956 (as amended). Any person or persons who do any
unauthorised act in relation to this publication may be liable to criminal
prosecution and civil claims for damages.

AD010606UK

Printed in the UK

CONTENTS

INTRODUCTION

KILL OR CURE

When we are ill or injured, we are at our most vulnerable. We put ourselves in the hands of doctors and nurses, trusting in their training, ability, experience and good will. Their procedures are often a mystery to us. They are often dangerous even in the hands of the most benign practitioner and, when a syringe is produced, we have little knowledge of what is being injected into us.

Consequently, while under the care of the medical profession, our lives are often in danger. But there are some doctors and nurses who deliberately go out to kill their patients. Those usually seen as Angels of Mercy turn into Angels of Death. Some relish acting as God, deciding who will live and who will die. Others see little point in allowing those who are elderly or terminally ill to continue living, eating up time and resources, when the outcome is not in doubt. A patient can simply be too troublesome and demanding to warrant further care and conveniently despatched. This may not necessarily be done with evil intent. In earlier times, it was seen as merciful for a doctor or nurse simply to ease a patient into the next life by the judicious administration of an overdose.

There are inadequates who relish being seen as heroes. They seek to push their patients to the brink of death, then, at the last moment, save them. This satisfies the illusion that they are indispensable to the patient and the institution. Endangering the lives of the patients will give them a sense of superiority over the doctors and other medical staff, whose knowledge and experience makes them feel inferior. This is a risky strategy and sometimes they fail to revive the victim. These people suffer from what is known as Munchausen's Syndrome by Proxy, where the primary carer gains kudos for looking after a patient who is at death's door. Again, if the condition is induced by the carer, things can go wrong.

Then there are those who are motivated by money. Numerous villains in Agatha Christie novels kill to benefit from the deceased's will, and such nefarious individuals exist in the real world, too. In some cases, doctors and nurses have used their position to persuade their wards to make them a beneficiary before bumping them off. Some kill simply for the thrill of it.

This, of course, is rare. There is no reason to be fearful next time you go to the doctor or have to spend time in hospital. But it does happen and doctors and nurses are proud of their profession. They know that those in their care are often likely to die in the hands of colleagues. When patients do die, other healthcare professionals do not immediately cast around looking for someone to blame.

Being motivated by the highest calling themselves, they do not easily impute malicious intent to others. Medical professionals naturally ascribe the highest of motives to coworkers. They find it difficult to imagine that a colleague is deliberately killing those they are supposed to look after, especially in intensive care wards where the death rate is naturally high. It is also hard for the loved ones of patients to suspect their carers. We naturally trust doctors and nurses. This means that often a case of murder is passed off as merely another unexpected death. The murders can often reach double or even triple figures before a killing spree is detected – if at all.

However – as this book shows – doctors and nurses do kill, deliberately, for multiple reasons. But then, we must accept that seeking medical help is often a matter of life or death.

MARY ANN COTTON

Mary Ann Cotton was the most prolific serial killer in Victorian England. Among her victims were her mother, a lover, a friend, three husbands and numerous stepchildren. It is thought that she killed ten of her own children.

Her life began in Dickensian surroundings. She was born Mary Ann Robson, in October 1832, within Low Moorsley, a small village located not far from the city of Sunderland in northeast England. Consisting of herself, two younger siblings and Mary Ann's parents, the Robson family was not a large one. However, her father, a miner, seems to have been forever struggling to make ends meet. His life above ground was devoted to his two beliefs: Methodism and the idea that children must be raised with a firm hand.

When Mary Ann was eight, her father moved the family to nearby Murton, where he was employed by the South Hetton Coal Company. Any advancement the family had hoped to make through the relocation soon vanished after he fell 45 m (148 ft) to his death down a mine shaft.

Six years later in 1846, Mary Ann's mother remarried. Although her stepfather had none of the financial worries that had plagued her father, the two men had at least one thing in common: the belief in strict discipline. At 16, Mary Ann escaped the family home by obtaining a position as a private nurse. She returned to her mother and stepfather three years later, but only for a brief period. Within months, a pregnant Mary Ann married William Mowbray, a labourer, and left the family home for good.

The young couple lived a somewhat transient lifestyle as Mowbray pursued work in the mines and in railway construction. Ultimately, they ended up where they had begun: in Sunderland, where Mowbray found work first as a foreman with the South Hetton Coal Company, then as a fireman aboard the steamer *Newburn*. In January 1865, Mowbray died of what was described as an intestinal disorder. Mary Ann received an insurance payment of £35 on his life. Wishing to express his condolences, the attending doctor revisited the house, surprising the widow who was dancing around the room in an expensive new dress.

Mary Ann Cotton buried three husbands, a prospective sister-in-law, a 'paramour', her mother and no fewer than 12 children.

During their 13-year marriage, Mary Ann and William Mowbray had nine children, only two of whom were still alive when their father died.

After Mowbray's death, Mary Ann moved eight kilometres south to Seaham Harbour. She began a relationship with Joseph Nattrass, a man who was engaged to another woman. It was at this point that one of her two remaining children, a three-year-old girl, died. After Nattrass married, Mary Ann returned to Sunderland with Isabella, her only surviving child. The girl was sent to live with her grandmother, and Mary Ann found employment with the Sunderland Infirmary House of Recovery for the Cure of Contagious Fever, Dispensary and Humane Society. While working there, she met an engineer named George Ward, who was suffering from a fever. His recovery was swift. Ward was discharged and, in August 1865, the two married. However, his ill-health returned soon after the wedding. During much of the marriage, he suffered from a lingering illness. Symptoms included paralyses and chronic stomach problems. When Ward died in October 1866, Mary Ann accused her late husband's doctor of malpractice.

As she had immediately after the death of her first husband, Mary Ann again left Sunderland. She settled in Pallion, where she was hired by a man named James Robinson. A shipwright, Robinson had also recently lost a spouse, and was in need of a housekeeper to look after his five children. But in December 1866, tragedy again struck the Robinson household when the youngest child died suddenly of gastric fever. Meanwhile Mary Ann, it seems, provided something more than sympathy for her new employer – she was soon with child.

Early in the New Year, Mary Ann received news that her mother had been taken ill. She made the trek back to Sunderland, arriving to find that her mother had all but recovered her health. Yet nine days later, she was dead.

With Isabella in tow, Mary Ann returned to her employer. Soon after their arrival, the girl began complaining of stomach pains, as did two of the Robinson children. By the end of April, all three were dead.

It can be said with some certainty that Robinson initially made no connection between the rash of deaths and his new housekeeper, for in August 1867 the two were married. The child Mary Ann was carrying, a daughter they named Mary Isabella, was born in late November. She lived for only three months.

The death of Mary Isabella proved to be the saddest event in a disastrous marriage. Although the couple would have one more child, the relationship deteriorated rapidly. Robinson soon came to the realization that his wife was running up debts without his knowledge and had stolen money he had asked her to deposit in the bank. After valuables began disappearing from the house, he confronted his children and was told that their stepmother had forced them to pawn the items. In late 1869, two years after they'd married, Mary Ann's husband threw her out of the house.

By the beginning of 1870, Mary Ann had been reduced to living on the streets. Her luck began to change when a friend, Margaret Cotton, introduced Mary Ann to her brother, Frederick. As in the case of Robinson, Frederick Cotton had been recently widowed. He'd also suffered through the deaths of two of his four children. Within a few months of meeting Mary Ann, he buried another child, who died of an apparent stomach ailment. Not long into the grieving process, Mary Ann became pregnant with Cotton's child. Early in the pregnancy, Margaret Cotton died of an ailment similar to that which had taken the life of her young nephew. Although Mary Ann was still married to Robinson – a secret she kept from the expectant father – she and Cotton were married in September 1870.

Shortly after the birth of her 11th child, a boy named Robert, Mary Ann heard news of Joseph Nattrass, her former lover. No longer married, Nattrass was living in the village of West Aukland, a little over 60 kilometres to the south. Not only did Mary Ann quickly move to resume the relationship, she somehow succeeded in convincing her husband to relocate the family closer to where Nattrass lived.

Two days after his first wedding anniversary, Cotton died from a gastric fever.

Shortly after her husband's death, Mary Ann welcomed Nattrass into her home as a 'lodger'. Although she had received a substantial payment owing from Cotton's life insurance policy, she went to work as a nurse for John Quick-Manning, an excise officer who was recovering from smallpox. She soon became pregnant by him.

Between 10 March and 1 April, death visited the Cotton home on three separate occasions. The first to die was Frederick Cotton, Jr. His death was followed by Robert, the child of Mary Ann and her late husband. Before the infant could be buried, Joseph Nattrass also died; but only after rewriting his will so that all would be left to Mary Ann.

Once again pregnant, this time with Quick-Manning's child, Mary Ann's thoughts turned to marriage. It would appear that to her thinking only one obstacle remained: Charles, the surviving Cotton child. Mary Ann had hoped that he might be sent to a workhouse, but was told by Thomas Riley, a minor parish official, that she would be obliged to accompany him.

After declining, she informed Riley that Charles was sickly, adding, 'I won't be troubled long. He'll go like all the rest of the Cottons.' Riley, who had always seen the boy healthy, thought the statement peculiar. When Charles Cotton died five days later, he visited the village authorities and urged an investigation.

An inquest held the following Saturday determined that Charles had, indeed, died of natural causes. Mary Ann's story that Riley had made the accusation because she had spurned his advances would very likely have affected his position as well as his reputation, had it not been for the local press.

Reporters looking into Mary Ann's story discovered that she had buried three husbands, a prospective sister-in-law, a paramour, her mother and no fewer than 12 children, nearly all of whom had died of stomach ailments. The revelations caused the doctor who had attended

Charles to reopen his investigation. He soon discovered traces of arsenic in the small samples he'd kept from the boy's stomach.

Mary Ann was arrested, and the body of Charles Cotton was exhumed. After another six corpses were dug up in failed attempts to locate the body of Joseph Nattrass, it was decided that she would stand trial for the murder of Charles alone. Proceedings were delayed a few months until the delivery of the baby fathered by Quick-Manning.

During the trial, Mary Ann attempted to explain Charles's death by saying that he had inhaled arsenic contained in the dye of the wallpaper of the Cotton home. The theory was dismissed and she was sentenced to death.

On 24 March 1873, Mary Ann Cotton was hanged at Durham County Gaol. Her death was long and painful, the result of an elderly hangman having miscalculated the required drop.

THOMAS NEILL CREAM

Doctor Thomas Neill Cream is thought to have been responsible for the deaths of at least eight women and one man, yet it is for something that may have happened during his last second of life that he is best remembered. Sentenced to hang for the murder of a 27-year-old prostitute, on 16 November 1892 Cream stood silent and calm at the gallows at Newgate Prison. Then, quite suddenly, he is said to have uttered: 'I am Jack...'

His final words were cut short when the trapdoor opened and the hangman's noose broke his neck. To some, Cream's statement was a confession that he was the murderer known as Jack the Ripper.

Cream's journey to justice appears long, twisted, and peculiar – even when compared to those of other serial killers. He was born in Glasgow on 27 May 1850, the eldest of eight children. Four years later, the growing family migrated to Wolfe's Cove, a small community not far from Quebec City, Canada. There, his father, William Cream, worked at a shipbuilding and lumber company before establishing the Cream Lumber Mill.

As the years passed, all the Cream boys would work in the mill. But Thomas was different from his brothers. A handsome young man, more interested in books than business, he left the mill in September

1872, enrolling in medicine at Montreal's McGill University. Montreal was then the largest, wealthiest and most powerful city in the country. McGill held a position of similar stature within the world of academe. It was considered Canada's foremost institution of learning, with a faculty of medicine that ranked among the most respected in North America.

A studious, if unexceptional student, within four years Cream graduated with a degree in medicine from McGill. At his convocation, he sat and listened as the dean delivered an address entitled 'The Evils of Malpractice in the Medical Profession'. Immediately after the ceremony, Cream was confronted by the family of Flora Brooks, a teenage girl he had been courting. Flora had been taken ill shortly after Cream's last visit to the family's hotel in the rural Quebec town of Waterford. She was then examined by a local physician named Phelan, who determined that she had recently undergone an abortion. Confronted, Flora confessed that it was Cream who had performed the operation.

Unwillingly, Cream was taken back to Waterford, where a hasty wedding ceremony was performed. Flora's honeymoon, however, was brief. She awoke the next morning to find her groom gone. Cream left nothing but a letter in which he promised to keep in touch.

The doctor made for London, England, where he registered at St Thomas's Hospital. Cream hoped to gain the training and experience required to become a surgeon, but failed to pass the entrance requirements for the Royal College of Surgeons. He achieved greater success at the Royal College of Surgeons in Edinburgh, where he earned a licence in midwifery.

It had been over a year since Cream had left his bride. While he had broken his marriage vows, the doctor had kept his promise to keep in touch. More than simple letters, he had been sending Flora medicine – which she dutifully took. After becoming ill, she was again examined by Dr Phelan who, upon learning of the mysterious prescription, advised her to ignore Cream's instructions. Although she rallied briefly, in August 1877 Flora Cream died of what was officially described as 'consumption'.

One year after the death of his wife, Cream returned to Canada. He set up practice in London, Ontario, over 700 kilometres away from Montreal.But it wasn't long before he was again involved in a scandal. In May 1879, the body of one of his patients, a waitress named Kate Gardener, was discovered in a woodshed behind the building in which he had his office. Upon investigation, it was discovered that the unmarried woman had gone to the doctor in the hope of obtaining an abortion.

Cream stated that this was true, adding that he had refused her request. He argued that her death, the result of an overdose of chloroform, was a suicide. A subsequent inquest disproved the doctor's theory – no bottle containing the chemical was found on the scene, and Gardener's face had been badly scratched, indicating a struggle. Although there appeared to be no evidence that he had committed the crime, suspicion fell on Cream, leaving his practice in ruins.

In the summer of 1879, he moved to the United States, settling in Chicago, where he was obliged to take the state board of health exam. The day after receiving his passing grade, Cream set up practice in an area just outside the city's red-light district. As his practice focused almost exclusively on providing abortions, it was a most convenient location. Most of the illegal operations were performed in rooms rented specifically for the purpose by a series of midwives he had recruited. When one of his patients, a prostitute named Mary Anne Faulkner, died, Cream's lawyer managed to convince a jury that the good doctor had arrived on the scene in an attempt to save the victim of a botched abortion.

Poisonous prescription

Within months, Cream again attracted the attention of the authorities when another patient, Ellen Stack, died after being prescribed antipregnancy pills. The medicine, assumed to have been of the doctor's own design, included strychnine among its ingredients. This poison also played a role in the death of his first male victim, a railway agent named Daniel Stott, with whose wife Cream was having an affair. When the husband came to suspect the infidelity, Cream added strychnine to the medicine he had prescribed for the man's epilepsy.

Cream might have again escaped justice were it not for his fear that the man's death could somehow rebound on him. Intent on avoiding this possibility, he wrote a letter to the coroner in which he accused a local pharmacist of having added strychnine to Stott's medicine. However, after the railway agent's body was exhumed, and the presence of the poison discovered, it was upon Cream that suspicion fell. He fled, only to be caught in the town of Bell River, Ontario, 30 kilometres within the Canadian border.

Betrayed by Mrs Stott, who testified against her former lover in November 1881, Cream was sentenced to life in Joliet State Penitentiary. As the years passed, his brother Daniel worked for Cream's release, a job made easier by a rather sizeable inheritance left to both men upon the passing of their father. Daniel Cream used Thomas's share of the money to ingratiate himself with a number of senior Illinois politicians. The ploy worked and, on 21 July 1891, Cream received a pardon from the governor of Illinois, Joseph W. Fifer.

It was an aged, weakened Cream who travelled back to Quebec in order to collect the balance of his inheritance. In September, he set sail for Liverpool. Cream arrived in London, very much a changed man from the handsome young doctor who had once walked its streets. He suffered from poor eyesight and persistent headaches, which he attempted to alleviate through the ingestion of low-grade morphine. As 'Thomas Neill, MD', he passed himself off as a resident doctor from St Thomas's, the very same hospital at which he had practised some 14 years earlier. It was under this cover that his greatest string of murders began.

The first victim was Nellie Donworth, a 19-year-old prostitute who was seen with a man matching Cream's description in the early evening of 13 October 1891. Before the night was out she would die an agonizing death from strychnine poisoning. Seven days later, Cream poisoned another prostitute, 27-year-old Matilda Clover, using gelatine pills containing strychnine. She endured a night of great pain before dying the following morning. However, her death was not recorded as murder; rather her physician believed she had died from a lethal mixture of liquor and a sedative he had prescribed to help combat her alcoholism.

In late 1891, Cream began a courtship with Laura Sabbatini, an attractive would-be designer of dresses. Their relationship endured a four-month separation, during which Cream was obligated to return to Canada in order to finally settle his father's estate. Whether his murder spree continued in the Dominion has always been a matter of speculation. What is known is that upon his return he attempted to poison a prostitute, Lou Harvey, with the claim that his gelatine pills of strychnine prevented pregnancy. However, she grew suspicious of the doctor and only pretended to take the pills. Two other prostitutes, Alice Marsh and Emma Shrivell, were less fortunate. On 11 April 1892, both suffered painful deaths in the hours after Cream left their shared flat.

Given that his only murder conviction came after he had attempted to pin the crime on another, it seems rather extraordinary that during this time Cream embarked on a similar campaign. Shortly after the murder of Nellie Donworth, he mailed two pseudonymous letters in which he accused Frederick Smith of W. H. Smith and Son of the murder. During his brief return to Canada he had printed a circular, warning patrons of London's Metropole Hotel that the murderer was employed at the hotel. Four weeks after the deaths of Marsh and Shrivell, the Deputy Coroner George Percival received a letter from a 'William H. Murray' in which it was claimed that Dr Walter Harper of St Thomas's Hospital was responsible for the murders. That same day, Walter Harper's father, Dr Joseph Harper, received an extortion letter in which the same claim was repeated. Detectives at Scotland Yard were quick to recognize that the same hand was behind all these documents, but were unable to determine the writer's identity. Their curiosity was raised further after two prominent Londoners received extortion letters in which one 'M. Malone' claimed to have evidence that each had carried out the murder of Matilda Clover – the victim whose death had been ruled accidental.

The beginning of the end for Cream came in April 1892 when, quite by chance, he befriended an expatriate American named John Haynes. As a former New York City detective, Haynes had taken an interest in Alice Marsh and Emma Shrivell, whose murders had occurred only a few nights earlier. As he discussed the case with Cream, Haynes was taken aback by the depth of information the doctor possessed. It seemed to the former detective that the doctor knew details that had not been reported. What was more, Cream linked the murders with those of two other women, Matilda Clover and Lou Harvey, whose names meant nothing to Haynes. After he had passed on this information to a friend at Scotland Yard, the body of Matilda Clover was exhumed. While they were still gathering evidence, on 3 June 1892, the London constabulary arrested Cream on suspicion of blackmail. Cream appeared at the inquest into Matilda Clover's death, obliged to listen to the damning testimony. Among the witnesses was Lou Harvey, who, until the moment she entered the courtroom, Cream had thought he'd killed. The inquest concluded that Cream had intentionally administered a lethal dose of strychnine to Matilda Clover. The same witnesses were called by the prosecution during the subsequent criminal trial. No one spoke in Cream's defence. It took the jury only ten minutes to deliver their verdict.

Infamous last words

But what of Cream's final words: 'I am Jack...'? It must first be said that there is some debate as to whether they were ever actually uttered, though his executioner, James Billington, swore it as fact. Assuming Cream did make the statement – and that what he had meant to say is 'I am Jack the Ripper' – is it at all possible that the Canadian doctor was the Ripper? At first glance, the answer must be negative. During the latter half of 1888, at which time Jack the Ripper committed his murders, Cream was serving the seventh year of his life sentence at Joliet State Penitentiary, across the Atlantic. Supporters of the theory that Cream was Jack the Ripper claim that corruption was such that the doctor left the institution years before receiving his official pardon. Another more complicated theory argues that Cream had a double who sat in the prison while Cream roamed the streets of London's East End.

Perhaps the best explanation for Cream's words can be found in his considerable ego. Might it have been such that Cream desired to claim the most notorious crimes of the day as his own?

H. H. HOLMES

I t is not correct, as is often claimed, that H. H. Holmes was America's first serial killer; both the Bloody Benders (a Kansas family of serial killers) and the Servant Girl Annihilator preceded him. He did, however, kill more people than the Servant Girl Annihilator and all the members of the Bender family put together. The claim that Holmes was the most prolific American serial killer of all time remains an issue of some debate.

The man who history remembers as H. H. Holmes was born Herman Webster Mudgett on 16 May 1860 in Gilmanton, New Hampshire. Nearly a century and a half later, the town numbers barely more than 3,000 inhabitants. It is perhaps most famous as having served as a model for Grace Metalious's Peyton Place, the setting for the 1956 novel of the same name.

Holmes grew up in an impoverished family with an abusive alcoholic father at its head. School provided only a partial escape. While an intelligent and handsome boy, he was also a frequent victim of bullying. He once claimed that, as a child, he had been forced by his classmates to touch a human skeleton. It was an event that appeared to haunt him for the rest of his life. Nevertheless, he sought to become a medical doctor and developed a fascination with anatomy. As an adolescent, this interest found expression in his killing and dismembering of stray animals.

At 16, he graduated from school and managed to get teaching positions – first in Gilmanton and later in nearby Alton, New Hampshire. It was there that he met Clara Lovering. The ardour between them was such that the two eloped. However, in marriage that same passion quickly dissipated and he soon abandoned his wife.

Still intent on a career in medicine, he attended the University of Vermont. It was, however, too small for his liking. In September 1882, he enrolled at the University of Michigan at Ann Arbor, which held what was considered to be one of the country's leading medical schools. Two years later, he graduated with what are best described as lacklustre grades.

After graduation, Mudgett adopted as his name the more distinguished sounding Henry Howard Holmes. He took up a position as prescription clerk in a pharmacy owned by a terminally ill doctor named Holton. He endeared himself to Holton's wife and customers. When the good doctor passed away, Holmes offered to buy the pharmacy, promising the newly made widow $100 a month. After signing over the deed, Mrs Holton subsequently disappeared; Holmes claimed she had settled with relatives in California.

Castle of death

Under Holmes, the pharmacy thrived in the growing Englewood neighbourhood of Chicago. In 1887, he married Myrta Z. Belknap, a stunning young woman whom he had met during a business trip to Minneapolis. She remained unaware that Holmes had been married before – and that he had not obtained a divorce. In their third year of marriage, Myrta bore a daughter named Lucy. By this time she had already returned to the home of her parents. Though Holmes would never seek a divorce, the union was all but over.

Holmes disfigured cadavers to make it appear that they had died in horrific accidents.

Using the pharmacy as his base, Holmes continued to engage in a number of questionable business ventures he had begun several years before. However, his most notable achievement was the construction of a block-long, three-storey building on the site across the street from his pharmacy. Built over a three-year period, 'The Castle', as the locals dubbed it, included a ground floor which Holmes rented out to various shopkeepers. The upper two storeys Holmes kept for himself. A huge space, it was a confusing maze of over a hundred windowless rooms, secret passageways, false floors and stairways that led to nowhere. Some doors could only be opened from the outside, while others opened to reveal nothing but a brick wall. During construction, Holmes repeatedly changed contractors, ensuring that no one understood the design of the building or had any idea as to its ultimate purpose.

Beginning shortly after the completion of the Castle, and for the three years that followed, Holmes murdered dozens of women. Some he tortured in soundproof chambers fitted with gas lines that enabled him to asphyxiate his victims. The corpses were sent down a secret chute to the Castle's basement. There, Holmes would dissect them, just as he had the animals he killed in his adolescence. They would be stripped of flesh and sold as skeleton models to medical schools. Some bodies were cremated or thrown in pits of lime and acid.

One of the first to die was Julia Connor, the wife of a jeweller to whom Holmes had rented a shop. After she came to Holmes with the news that she was pregnant with his child, the doctor murdered Julia and her daughter, Pearl.

Holmes saw great opportunity in Chicago's upcoming 1893 World's Columbian Exposition and made several modifications to the second storey of the Castle, transforming it into the World's Fair Hotel. The first guests arrived in the spring of 1893. Some returned home, others did not. With the high volume of guests, Holmes could be selective in choosing his victims. The fact that so many people were coming to the fair without any place to stay ensured that his activities went unnoticed.

One of those who remained alive was Georgiana Yorke, who became Holmes's third wife in January 1894. She believed Holmes to be a very wealthy man, with property in Texas and Europe. Indeed, he appeared to be quite prosperous. However, his debts had begun to catch up with him.

Running out of time

After having been confronted by his creditors, he came up with a scheme which involved a man named Benjamin Pietzel. As a carpenter, Pietzel had worked on the Castle. Exactly how much he knew of Holmes's activities is a matter of some debate. What is certain is that Pietzel agreed to fake his own death in order to collect a large insurance claim. In the end, Holmes simply killed the man and kept all the money for himself. He then made off with three of Pietzel's children.

On 17 November 1894, having been on the road for nearly two years, Holmes was arrested in Boston. Initially, he was suspected of nothing more than fraud. However, an insurance agent's diligence in attempting to track down the three Pietzel children revealed that they had been killed in the cities of Indianapolis and Toronto. This news encouraged the police in Chicago to investigate Holmes's Castle. On 20 July 1895, all was revealed. The police spent a month investigating what some now called 'the Murder Castle' before, on 19 August, it was consumed by a fire of mysterious origin.

Exactly how many poor souls Holmes murdered is a mystery. The number has typically been estimated as being between 20 and 100. The authorities put the murder count at 27, committed in Chicago, Philadelphia, Indianapolis and Toronto. The police in Chicago noted that many of the bodies in the basement of the Castle had been dissected and burnt to such an extent that it was difficult to determine precisely how many bodies it contained. At his trial, Holmes confessed to 27 murders.

Holmes was led to the gallows on the morning of 7 May 1896. As he watched the preparations for his hanging, he is reported to have said, 'Take your time; don't bungle it.' However, despite the hangman's care, Holmes died an agonizing death. For ten minutes after the trapdoor was sprung, his body twitched. He was officially pronounced dead after he had been hanging for 15 minutes.

AMELIA DYER

A t 11 a.m. on the morning of 30 March 1896, William Povey was walking along the riverbank at Sonning, where the River Kennet joins the Thames near Reading, when he saw a woman carrying a brown paper parcel tucked under her cloak. Later, he saw the woman returning without the parcel. A bargeman named Charles Humphreys then spotted a brown paper parcel floating in shallow water.

When he caught hold of it with his punt-hook to pull it into his boat, the wet paper tore and a baby's leg stuck out. He reported his find to the police, who came to collect it.

Dr William Maurice opened the parcel in the mortuary and found it contained the body of a baby girl with a white tape knotted around her neck and a brick.

The paper wrapped around the child's body had on it a label from Bristol Temple Meads railway station and a name and address: 'Mrs Thomas, 26 Piggott's Road, Lower Caversham.'

A clerk at the station confirmed that a parcel had been delivered to Mrs Thomas at 26 Piggott's Road, but she had since moved to 45 Kensington Road in nearby Reading, where she was living as Mrs Harding.

Baby Doris's fate

Meanwhile, an advertisement had appeared in the *Bristol Times and Mirror*. It read: 'MARRIED couple with no family would adopt healthy child, nice country home. Terms, £10 – Harding, care of Ship's Letter Exchange, Stokes Croft, Bristol.'

Alongside it was another small advertisement that read: 'NURSE CHILD – Wanted, respectable woman to take young child at home – State terms to Mrs Scott, 23 Manchester Street, Cheltenham.'

Mrs Scott was, in fact, 23-year-old barmaid Evelina Edith Marmon, a single mother who was not in a position to support her three-month-old baby daughter, Doris.

She hoped to find someone to take care of her child for a weekly fee in the hope that, if her circumstances changed, she could reclaim her later.

During the Victorian era 'baby farming' was a common phenomenon. Unmarried women risked ruin if they had a child, so others would take them in, either for a regular stipend or a flat fee. Unfortunately, those who took a flat fee had little incentive to spend money on their wards and some simply killed off the children in their care as soon as the fee was paid.

Evelina exchanged letters with Mrs Harding, who assured her: 'Myself and my husband are dearly fond of children. I have no child of my own. A child with me will have a good home and a mother's love and care. We belong to the Church of England.' In fact, Mrs Harding, whose real name was Amelia Dyer, had long separated from her husband and had two children – a son and a daughter – of her own. She said she would take baby Doris for a flat fee of £10 (worth an estimated £1,300/$1,700 today). There would be no further expenses.

The day after the body of the baby girl had been fished from the Thames, Mrs Dyer went to Cheltenham to collect Doris, along with her baby clothes, which were packed in a carpetbag. She took the £10 and assured Evelina that she could visit Doris whenever she wished.

From there, Dyer took Doris on the train to Paddington, arriving at 9 p.m. She then took the omnibus to 76 Mayo Road, Willesden, where her daughter Mary Ann – known as Polly – lived with her husband Alfred Palmer. A woman named Ann Beattie offered to carry the carpetbag for her. She saw a young woman waiting by the door. Inside, Dyer knotted a white ribbon around Doris's neck and strangled her.

'Dear little boy' strangled

Mrs Harding's small ad also appeared in the *Weekly Despatch*, where it was seen by Amelia Sargeant, an undertaker's wife who had six children of her own. She was also caring for 13-month-old Harry Simmonds for six shillings (30p, the equivalent of £38/$50 now) a week. However, his mother had wanted Harry to be adopted. Mrs Sargeant found keeping him a struggle so Mrs Harding's advertisement seemed to be the answer.

She replied to the advertisement and got an answer from Mrs Harding, at 45 Kensington Road, Reading, saying she would be happy to take the 'dear little boy'.

'I have no child of my own,' she said. 'He would be well brought up and have a mother's love and care.'

In further correspondence, Mrs Harding said she was actually Mrs Thomas, but did not want to advertise under her own name. Mrs Sargeant visited 45 Kensington Road, which was clean and comfortable, and she agreed that Mrs Thomas should have the child for a flat fee. However, she was not to bring him to Reading. Instead, the handover should take place at Paddington Station.

The day after Mrs Dyer had turned up with Doris, she and a woman she said was her niece met Mrs Sargeant and her husband at Paddington. They were accompanied by a child named Harold. Mrs Sargeant handed over Harry, along with £5, and said the remaining £5 would be paid in ten days' time. She also said she would send Harry's clothes when she got home.

Back at Mayo Road, Mrs Dyer put Harold to bed, but when he began to cry Mrs Dyer strangled him too. That evening, seemingly without a care in the world, she went with her daughter and son-in-law to see the Sporting and Military Show at Olympia. The Palmers slept soundly that night and Mrs Dyer settled down again on the couch, but in the small hours she was awoken by what she thought was the sound of a baby crying. Checking under the couch she found that the two small packages containing the dead children were quite still.

The following afternoon, Mrs Dyer packed the two little bundles into a carpetbag, adding two bricks from the next-door neighbour's garden. Her daughter and son-in-law accompanied her to Paddington, where she caught the 9.15 p.m. train to Reading, arriving there at 10.05 p.m. It was raining as she lugged the heavy bag down the dark streets to the river. After she had made sure there was nobody about, she dropped the bag into the water from the Clappers footbridge. As she hurried home, she was spotted by John Toller, an engineer from Reading Gaol. He said she was empty-handed.

Decomposing body in cupboard

The police investigating the baby's body found in the river discovered that Mrs Harding was in the business of adopting children, so they sent a young woman to 45 Kensington Road. Mrs Harding was not there, but she was greeted by an old lady who identified herself as 'Granny Smith'. She told the young woman to come back two days later. When she returned, Mrs Harding agreed to adopt a child, which she should bring 'tomorrow evening after dark'. Instead, Detective Sergeant Harry James and Constable James Anderson arrived at the front door. They showed Mrs Harding the brown paper that had wrapped the baby's body, which bore her name and previous address, but she could offer no explanation. She claimed that she had received a package when she was living at Caversham and had put the wrapping paper in the bin with the rest of the rubbish.

Under questioning, Mrs Harding revealed that her real name was Dyer, though she sometimes used the name Thomas, which was the surname of her first husband. A search of the house revealed piles of babywear, pawn tickets for children's clothing which had not been redeemed and correspondence concerning the adoption of children for money. Far worse, a stench coming from a cupboard indicated that a body had been left there to decompose before being disposed of. Then in a sewing basket the police found white tape, similar to that found around the neck of the child fished from the Thames, and macramé string like that tied around the parcel.

Dyer was then arrested and at the police station she produced a small pair of scissors and tried to harm herself. They had to be wrested from her. She then tried to strangle herself with a lace from her boots.

The amount of children's clothing found in Dyer's house indicated that there were probably other victims, so the police set about dragging the river. They found the bodies of seven children, but only two could be identified. They were those of Doris Marmon and Harry Simmonds, who were identified by Evelina Marmon and Amelia Sargeant.

Confessing, Dyer said: 'You'll know mine by the tape around their necks.'

Gaol confession

Dyer was then charged with the murder of the children. The police also visited Mayo Road, where the bricks used to weigh down the bag were identified by the Palmers' landlord, who had been moving a fire grate. Arthur Palmer and Polly were charged as accomplices, but Dyer made a confession from Reading Gaol, exonerating them. Addressed to Superintendent Tewsley and dated 16 April 1896, it read, with spelling and punctuation as the original:

> Sir will you kindly grant me the favour of presenting this to
> the magistrates on Saturday the 18th instant I have made

this statement out, for I may not have the oportunity then I must releive my mind I do know and I feel my days are numbered on this earth but I do feel it is an awful thing drawing innocent people into trouble I do know I shal have to answer before my Maker in Heaven for the awful crimes I have committed but as God Almighty is my judge in Heaven as on Hearth neither my daughter Mary Ann Palmer nor her husband Alfred Ernest Palmer I do most solemnly declare neither of them had any thing at all to do with it, they never knew I contemplated doing such a wicked thing until it was to late I am speaking the truth and nothing but the truth as I hope to be forgiven, I myself and I alone must stand before my Maker in Heaven to give a answer for it all witnes my hand Amelia Dyer.

Long career as baby farmer

Although charged with only two murders, Amelia Dyer had been in the baby-farming business for nearly 30 years. Born Amelia Hobley in Pyle Marsh, near Bristol in 1838, she had received a good education and served an apprenticeship as a corset maker. At 24 she married 57-year-old George Thomas and had to give up training as a nurse when she gave birth to a son. She also met midwife Ellen Dane, who took in unmarried pregnant women and worked as a baby farmer.

At the age of 31, Mrs Thomas found herself widowed. After farming out her own child, she went into baby farming on her own account, under the name of Mrs Harding. Then in 1872 she married William Dyer, an unskilled labourer. The following year, they had a daughter named Mary Ann, aka Polly. When her husband lost his job, Mrs Dyer went back into the baby-farming business. She offered a 'premium' service, which meant that after a one-off payment the mother would not be seeing the child again.

Women came to Dyer's house to give birth and numerous babies in her care were registered as 'stillborn'. One doctor became suspicious when the deaths of four infants were registered in two weeks. One of them was three-month-old May Walters, who died of malnutrition, weighing just 3kg (6½ lb). However, escaping prosecution for murder on a technicality, she was sentenced to six months' hard labour for causing death by neglect.

She then tried other trades but after moving house she went back into baby farming. One baby she took in was the child of a governess whose father was the son of her employer, which would normally have made marriage out of the question. The mother paid Dyer £15 to have the baby adopted, but after a few weeks she turned up to ensure that the child was being well cared for, only to be shown another infant which did not have her baby's distinctive birthmark.

When the mother demanded her baby back, Dyer evaded the issue by cutting her throat in a failed suicide bid and was sent to an insane asylum. When she was released, she moved and continued baby farming. By this time the family had relented and the couple had married, so they tracked down Dyer in search of their child. This time, Dyer attempted to overdose on laudanum, attacking a doctor who came to her aid with a poker. After another spell in the asylum, she tried drowning herself and was returned to the same institution. However, little could be found wrong with her, so she was sent to the workhouse.

Mystery of floating parcel solved

There she met Jane 'Granny' Smith, a penniless widow who had lost her children as well as her husband. They went into baby farming together, though they were forced to move when the newly formed National Society for the Prevention of Cruelty to Children took an interest. Smith did not seem to be puzzled when children suddenly went missing, having been found a 'good home', and nor was she surprised by the large amount of children's clothes that were pawned and never redeemed.

One of the children they took in was nine-year-old Willie Thornton, who brought with him an old carpetbag which he later identified as the bag containing the bodies of Doris Marmon and Harry Simmonds. For a while Arthur and Polly Palmer lived with them in Caversham, before Dyer, Smith and Willie moved to Reading and the Palmers moved to Willesden.

An advertisement in the *Western Daily Express* under the name 'Mrs Thornley' drew a response from May Fry, who had recently given birth to Helena. Thornley – that is, Dyer – agreed to take the child for £10 and collected her from Bristol Temple Meads station. At around 9 p.m., Dyer returned home with a brown paper parcel about two feet long and about a week later Smith noticed a bad smell coming from a cupboard. Soon afterwards, Dyer left the house with a brown paper parcel, saying she was going to pawn the contents.

The parcel contained the remains of Helena Fry, the baby discovered by Charles Humphreys, the bargeman. Her tragic end would be the key to unmasking a monster.

Found guilty and executed

At the Old Bailey, Dyer confessed to the murder of Helena Fry, along with those of Doris Marmon and Harry Simmonds, but pleaded insanity. This plea was dismissed and it took the jury less than five minutes to return a guilty verdict. She was hanged at Newgate Prison on 10 June 1897. The case gave a welcome boost to the NSPCC and the laws concerning adoption were tightened. Over her long career, Dyer may have killed as many as 300–400 children, making her one of the most prolific serial killers in history.

Arthur Palmer then appeared in court but was discharged. Later he was convicted of deserting a four-year-old girl in Devonport, where he and Polly were living under the name of Mr and Mrs Paton. Polly was to appear at a separate trial at the Berkshire Assizes in Reading and her lawyer took out a subpoena for Mrs Dyer to appear as a witness. However, the date of the hearing fell after her execution and the Home Secretary decided that the execution could not be delayed. He declared that the law must run its course and that Dyer was 'legally dead' from the time the death sentence had been pronounced. No evidence was presented at the assizes and Polly walked free.

Two years later, a three-week-old baby girl was found wrapped in a parcel under the seat of a railway carriage in a siding in Newton Abbot. The child was alive and had recently been adopted by a 'Mrs Stewart'. When Mrs Stewart was arrested, she turned out to be Dyer's daughter Polly.

JANE TOPPAN

Nurse and carer Jane Toppan said that her ambition had been 'to have killed more people – helpless people – than any other man or woman who ever lived'. In her 16-year career as a poisoner she certainly tried her best, killing maybe as many as 100. Her motive seems to have been sexual and her actions perhaps provoked by inherited insanity.

Born Nora Kelley in Boston in 1854, she was the daughter of Irish immigrants. She lost her mother Bridget to tuberculosis when an infant, leaving her and her siblings in the care of her abusive alcoholic father Peter who was known as 'Kelley the Crack' – crack as in crackpot. He went insane. He was reportedly found in his shop sewing his eyelids together. Nora's older sister Nellie later followed him to the asylum. Their grandmother was unable to look after the remaining children, so six-year-old Nora and her sister Delia, aged eight, were sent to the Boston Female Asylum, an orphanage for indigent girls.

At the age of ten, the orphanage placed their wards with respectable families. Nora and Delia were farmed out as indentured servants. Delia fell into prostitution, became an alcoholic and died in poverty. Nora was taken in by Abner and Ann Toppan, who changed Nora's name to

Jane and took her to live in Lowell, Massachusetts. While they never formally adopted her, she took their surname.

Because of prejudice against the Irish, the Toppans passed Jane off as an Italian whose parents had died at sea. Displaying the early hallmarks of a sociopath, Jane herself began telling outrageous lies. Her father, she said, had sailed around the world. Her sister married an English nobleman. Her brother was decorated at Gettysburg by Abraham Lincoln.

Brilliant and aggressive

Jane did well at school, graduating aged 18. But she was a mischievous child, prone to lying and petty theft, but very smart.

'In her school work, as in her profession in later years, she was one of the leaders of her class – brilliant and aggressive in all things,' a newspaper story said after her death.

The Toppans freed Jane from her indenture and gave her $50, but she stayed in the household as a servant. While Jane put on weight, it was her foster sister Elizabeth that was popular with the boys in Lowell. Nevertheless Jane got engaged, but when her fiancé went to find work 113 km (70 miles) away in Holyoke he married his landlady's daughter there. Jane hammered the engagement ring he'd given her to pieces. She then became withdrawn and twice tried to kill herself.

At the age of 26, she decided to study nursing at a hospital in Cambridge, Massachusetts, where she was hardworking and popular initially. There she became known as 'Jolly Jane' for her outgoing personality. However, she liked to gossip and celebrated the dismissal of students she didn't like. The lies continued. She said that the Tsar of Russia had offered her a nursing job. And she probably stole small things. Her fellow students grew to detest her.

The hospital administration were concerned about her ghoulish interest in autopsies. What they did not know was that, during her residency, she used her elderly patients as guinea pigs in experiments with drugs. She would alter their prescribed dosages to see what effect it had on their nervous systems. Seemingly an Angel of Mercy, she would spend a lot of time alone with her victims, making up fake charts and medicating them so that they would drift in and out of consciousness. She even got into bed with them.

Practice murders

When two patients under her care died in mysterious circumstances, she was fired. These early killings she said she considered 'practice murders'. She later admitted getting a sexual thrill from watching victims as they lost consciousness and would cradle them as they died. A patient named Amelia Phinney survived the bitter-tasting medicine Toppan had given her. She said that, as she lapsed into unconsciousness, Toppan climbed into bed with her and began kissing her all over the face. But something startled her and she stopped. The next morning Phinney decided it had all been a dream. Fourteen years later, when Jane Toppan was arrested, Phinney realized that it was no dream.

Jane went on to work at Massachusetts General Hospital in Boston, where she continued killing patients. Her method was to use a mixture of morphine and atrophine, the active ingredient in belladonna. Morphine made the pupils constrict, while atrophine made them dilate. A careful balance of them disguised the symptoms of poisoning. She discovered this method reading about the much publicized case of Dr Robert Buchanan of New York City who murdered his wife for the insurance money in 1892. He went to the electric chair in Sing Sing in July 1895.

By then Toppan had been dismissed by Massachusetts General for recklessly dispensing opiates. Nevertheless, doctors recommended her as a private nurse to their wealthy clients. Soon she was earning $25 a week, when the average weekly wage for a woman was $5. Outside of her job she guzzled beer, told dirty jokes, gossiped madly and enjoyed turning her friends against each other. But to the doctors and her patients she seemed a highly skilled professional, compassionate and cheerful.

Returning to Cambridge, her next two victims were Israel and Lovey Dunham, her elderly landlords. Mr Dunham died in May 1895, aged 83. The cause of death was give as a 'strangulated hernia'. Eighty-seven-year-old Mrs Dunham died two years later, reportedly of 'old age'. Toppan later explained they had become 'feeble and fussy' and 'old and cranky'. Her colleagues in nursing school remembered her saying there was no use keeping old people alive.

When wealthy widow Mary McNear, aged 70, fell ill on a visit to Cambridge, her doctor sent 'one of my best nurses' – Jane Toppan – to look after her. After just three hours of nursing, McNear died, apparently of 'apoplexy'. A month later, Toppan killed her old friend Myra Conners with strychnine so Jane could take over her job as the dining hall matron at St John's Theological School in Cambridge. But she was soon fired when financial irregularities were discovered.

Then, in 1899, Jane's foster sister Elizabeth, who was married to the deacon of the Lowell Church Oramel, Brigham invited her to visit. When Elizabeth complained of depression, Jane took her on a picnic consisting of cold corned beef, taffy and mineral water laced with strychnine.

'I held her in my arms and watched with delight as she gasped her life out,' Toppan said later.

The following year, she killed the widower's 45-year-old house-keeper Florence Calkins. The cause of death was given as 'chronic diabetes'.

Toppan's killing spree reached new heights in 1901. She poisoned new landlords Melvin and Eliza Beedle early that year, but only gave enough medication to make them ill. She then drugged their housekeeper, Mary Sullivan, to make her appear drunk so she could take her job. Then she killed the entire Davis family in two months that summer.

Mineral water

Jane was living a house rented from the Davis family at Cataumet, a neighbourhood of Bourne, Massachusetts, but could not keep up with the rent. When Mattie Davis turned up to collect it on a sweltering July day, Toppan gave her a glass of mineral water. She fell ill. Toppan nursed her over the next seven days, dosing her with morphine. By the time she died, her daughter Geraldine Gordon was ill and Mattie's widower, retired sea captain Alden Davis, begged her to stay on to nurse her. Geraldine died three weeks after her mother. Alden himself died two weeks later. The surviving daughter, Minnie Gibbs, refused to sign off the rental debt that Toppan owed the family. After drinking a tonic given to her by the nurse, Minnie died too.

When Minnie's husband, sailor Captain Paul Gibbs, returned from sea, he became suspicious that the entire, seemingly healthy, Davis family had perished so suddenly. He spoke to the police who called in toxicologist Leonard Wood and had the bodies exhumed. Investigation revealed that his wife died of morphine and atrophine poisoning.

Toppan then returned to Lowell, where she had designs on marrying Oramel Brigham, her step-sister's former partner. Within three days she killed his older sister, 77-year-old Edna Barrister, fearing she might oppose any match between them. She took over the running of the house from Edna and tried to impress Brigham with her housekeeping skills. Brigham made it clear he didn't want her as a housekeeper or as a wife.

Toppan decided to win his love by poisoning him, then nursing him back to health. That didn't work either, so she threatened to claim he'd made her pregnant. Enraged, Brigham ordered Toppan out of the house. She then tried to commit suicide with an overdose of morphine, but failed and went to the hospital. Upon her release, she went to the home of George Nichols in Amherst, New Hampshire, to nurse his sister Sarah. By then a Massachusetts state detective was on her tail, suspecting her of killing the entire Davis family. There, on 29 October

1901, she was arrested for the murder of Minnie Gibbs. She voluntarily returned to Massachusetts, though she continued protesting her innocence.

But when she was interviewed by a psychiatrist, she could not resist boasting about how many she had killed. In jail awaiting trial, she told newspaper men that she had given the consultant psychiatrist and the attorney general 'the names of 31 persons I killed, but, as a matter of fact, I killed many more whose names I cannot recall. I think it would be safe to say I killed at least a hundred from the time I became a nurse at Boston hospital, where I killed the first one, until I ended the lives of the Davis family'. However, only 12 murders were confirmed, though 100 were suspected.

'If all of the suspicions involving the operations of Jane Toppan could be substantiated in the opinion of men acquainted with the investigations in Cataumet, Cambridge and Lowell, the succession of murders will cover a wider range and be more astounding than any series of crimes perpetuated by one person in many years,' said the newspaper the *Lowell Sun* on 1 November 1901.

During her eight-hour trial on 23 June 1902, she was asked by her counsel 'how did you kill them?' Toppan replied: 'I gave them doses of morphine and atrophine tablets in mineral water and sometimes in a dilution of whiskey. Then I also used injections just as I did Cataumet. I do not remember how I killed them all, but those that I recall were poisoned by atrophine and morphine. My memory is not good; I forget some things. No, I have absolutely no remorse. I have never felt sorry for what I have done. Even when I poisoned my dearest friends, as the Davises were, I did not feel any regret afterward. I do not feel any remorse now. I have thought it all over, and I cannot detect the slightest bit of sorrow over what I have done.'

In a confession printed as a supplement to the *New York Journal*, she claimed her murderous ways were sparked by being dumped when she was 16 years old.

'If I had been a married woman, I probably would not have killed all of those people,' she said. 'I would have had my husband, my children and my home to take up my mind.'

Toppan was declared not guilty by reason of insanity and sent to Taunton State Hospital for life. When she initially came to the asylum she refused to eat, afraid that her food may be poisoned – which the newspapers gloated was an ironic revenge.

She died there at the age of 84 on 17 August 1938. Attendants remembered her calling them into her room and smiling. 'Get some morphine, dearie,' she would say, 'and we'll go out in the ward. You and I will have a lot of fun seeing them die.'

BELLE GUNNESS

Belle Gunness can lay serious claim to being the first female serial killer of modern times. She was the archetypal black widow killer, a woman who repeatedly attracted husbands and other suitors, and promptly murdered them for their money. While others, like Nannie Doss, were relatively timid murderers who would wait years for the chance to poison their latest husband, Belle was happy to despatch most of her suitors almost immediately and, if they did not care to take a drop of cyanide, she was quite willing to terminate their prospects with the blow from an axe or hammer. After all, at a strongly built 280 pounds, there were not too many men able to overpower her.

Belle Gunness may also have a second claim to fame. There are very few serial killers who have succeeded in evading the law even after being identified. The Hungarian Bela Kiss was one; Norwegian-born Belle Gunness was another.

Belle Gunness was born Brynhild Paulsdatter Storset on 11 November 1859 in the Norwegian fishing village of Selbu. Her parents had a small farm there and Belle's father also moonlighted as a conjuror. Allegedly Belle, in her youth, would appear alongside him as a tightrope walker and it is certainly true to say that she walked a tightrope for the rest of her life.

In 1883 her older sister, Anna, who had emigrated to Chicago, invited Belle to join her in the United States. Belle jumped at the chance of a new life and soon arrived in Chicago. The following year she married a fellow immigrant, Mads Sorenson. They lived together happily enough for the next decade or so. They failed to conceive children but instead fostered three girls, Jennie, Myrtle and Lucy. The only dramas to strike these hard-working immigrants were the regular fires that dogged their businesses. Twice their houses burnt down and, in 1897, a confectionery store they ran also succumbed to fire. Thankfully, each time they were well insured.

Insurance also served Belle well when, on 30 July 1900, Mads Sorenson died suddenly at home, suffering from what was officially listed as heart failure, but strangely showing all the symptoms of strychnine poisoning. Amazingly enough, he died on the day that one life insurance policy elapsed and another one started, so his grieving widow was able to claim on both policies.

Death by sausage grinder

With her $8,500 windfall, Belle decided to start a new life. She moved her family to the rural town of La Porte, Indiana, a place popular with Scandinavian immigrants, and soon married again, this time to Peter Gunness, a fellow Norwegian. Sadly, this marriage was not to last as long as her first. In 1903 Peter died in a tragic accident after a sausage grinder allegedly fell on his head. If some observed that it looked as if a hammer blow might have caused the head wound, the grieving – and pregnant – widow's tears were enough to quieten them. Once again there was an insurance payment, this time for $4,000.

Belle never married again, though not, it appears, for want of trying. She placed regular advertisements in the Norwegian language press's lonely hearts columns. Describing herself as a comely widow, she advertised for men ready to support their amorous advances with a solid cash investment in their future lives together. She received many replies and several of these suitors actually arrived in La Porte, cash or bankbooks in hand. They would be seen around town for a day or two, tell their loved ones they were preparing to marry a rich widow and then they would disappear.

They were not the only people around Belle to disappear. Her foster daughter Jennie also vanished – Belle told neighbours that she had gone to a finishing school in California. Farmhands seemed to go missing on the Gunness farm on a regular basis. As far as the community as a whole was concerned, however, Belle Gunness was a model citizen who had had some very bad luck.

This view seemed to be compounded once and for all when, on 28 April 1908, Belle's house caught fire. Fire-fighters were unable to stop the blaze in time and the bodies of two of Belle's three children were found in the rubble, along with an adult female body assumed to be that of Belle herself – though identification was difficult as the body had been decapitated. The beheaded body was clear evidence that this was no accident, but murder. The police immediately arrested an obvious suspect, local handyman Ray Lamphere, who had had an on/off relationship with Belle, but had lately fallen out with her and threatened to burn her house down.

That might have been the end of the matter if investigators had not continued digging around the site, looking for the corpse's missing head. They did not find the head but they did find 14 other corpses buried around the farm, mostly in the hog pen. Among those they were able to identify were two handymen, foster daughter Jennie and five of the hopeful suitors. The remainder were mostly presumed to be other unidentified suitors.

No ordinary widow

It was horribly clear that Belle Gunness was no ordinary widow but a vicious serial killer. More alarm bells rang when it was discovered that some of the bodies recovered from the fire had cyanide in their stomachs. Rumours immediately began to spread that the adult female corpse was not Belle. These were partially quashed a couple of weeks later, when her dental bridge and two teeth (looking suspiciously untouched by fire) were found in the rubble. Some accepted this as definitive evidence that Belle was dead. Others saw it as simply a final act of subterfuge. The prosecution of Ray Lamphere went ahead, but

Belle Gunness.

the jury expressed its doubts as to whether Belle was really dead by finding the handyman guilty only of arson and not of murder.

Sightings of Belle Gunness began almost immediately and continued in the ensuing years. Most of them were obviously wrong, and to this day the true story of the United States's first known female serial killer remains shrouded in mystery.

JEANNE WEBER

The neighbourhood of Goutte d'Or – Drop of Gold – in Paris was described by novelist Émile Zola as the 'dark theatre of sordid destinies'. Home to prostitutes and Apaches (bands of criminals), its reputation was not helped by serial child killer Jeanne Weber. Despite being dubbed 'The Ogress of the Goutte d'Or' by the press, she was repeatedly given the benefit of the doubt by credulous family members, employers, doctors and lawyers, which allowed her to kill and kill again. She strangled at least ten children – including three of her own – and maybe as many as 20.

Born Jeanne Marie Moulinet in the Breton fishing village of Paimpol on 2 October 1874, she cared for her younger brothers and sisters until she left home. According to her father, a fisherman from Iceland, she was very gentle with them. He also said that she was a good child who never gave her parents any trouble.

The family was poor and Jeanne was not very successful at school, so when she was 14 her parents gave her 25 francs – their entire savings – to go to Paris, which would relieve the family of one mouth to feed. She took various jobs, including working as a nanny to the five children of an architect living in Avenue de Clichy.

Deaths blamed on alcoholism

In La Chapelle, a district bordering the Goutte d'Or, she met her future husband, Jean Weber, a borderline alcoholic who worked as a timekeeper for a transport company. They married there on 2 June 1894. Her parents, now farmers in the Côtes-du-Nord (later Côtes-d'Armor), did not attend the wedding. Jeanne was pregnant at the time and their first child, Marcel Jean, was born five months later on 4 November. However, the baby died on 20 January 1895, aged almost three months. This was ascribed to husband Jean's drinking, which was thought at the time to have an adverse effect on any offspring. Jeanne was soon drinking heavily too.

A second son, Marcel Charles, was born on 9 January 1898 and a daughter, Juliette, came into the world on 3 January 1900. Juliette died on 22 January 1901, the cause of death being given as pneumonia. Again it was assumed that alcoholics would have unhealthy children, though Jeanne nevertheless sought consolation in the bottle.

Deadly babysitter

Their fortunes failing, the Webers then moved from La Chapelle to the Goutte d'Or, a downmarket area on the other side of the Northern Railroad tracks, where Jeanne sought work in childcare. She was soon looking after the infant Lucie, daughter of widower Alphonse Alexandre. The child fell ill while her father was out on Christmas Day 1902 and she died soon after he returned at 4 p.m. Again, the cause of death was given as pneumonia.

Then early in 1903 she went to work as a nanny for the Poyata family, who ran a dairy in the nearby Clignancourt district. One day she was found squeezing the lifeless body of three-year-old Marcelle Poyata and once again the death was ascribed to pneumonia. A few days later, Jeanne returned to the Poyata household, but immediately Marcelle's four-year-old brother Jacques took fright and ran away.

Jean Weber's family still lived in La Chapelle. On 2 March 1905 his sister-in-law Blanche wanted to do the laundry in a nearby public washhouse, so she left two-year-old Suzanne and 18-month-old Georgette, her daughters by Jean's brother Pierre, in the care of Jeanne. Soon a neighbour came to the washhouse to tell Blanche that Georgette was ill with convulsions. She rushed home to find the child lying red-faced on the bed and breathing with difficulty, while Jeanne had her hand on the infant's chest. However, when Blanche took hold of the child she was soon smiling again.

Blanche then returned to finish the laundry, leaving the children in Jeanne's care once more. When she returned, Georgette was dead. Madame Pouche, a neighbour, pointed out black and blue marks around the child's neck but, perhaps out of family loyalty, Pierre Weber chose to ignore them.

Nine days later, Jeanne was asked to look after Suzanne. When her parents returned, the child was dead and again there were bruises around her neck. The doctor informed the police, but they took no action and the two-year-old was buried without further ado.

On 26 March, Jeanne arrived unannounced at the house of her brother-in-law Léon Weber and helped herself to breakfast. As it happened, his wife Marie wanted to go out, so she asked Jeanne to babysit her seven-month-old daughter Germaine. Half an hour after Marie left the apartment, Germaine's grandmother, who lived downstairs, heard the child cry out.

She went upstairs to find the infant red-faced and breathing heavily. When she took Germaine from Jeanne, the child soon calmed and began breathing normally.

After the grandmother had returned to her flat, she heard Germaine cry out again.

Quickly returning to Léon and Marie's apartment, she found the child choking. However, when Jeanne left, leaving the infant with her grandmother, she soon revived. But Jeanne returned the following day and Germaine's parents blithely left the child in her care again. She was dead when they returned and the cause of death was given as diphtheria.

Marks around victim's neck

Three days later, on 29 March, while Germaine was being buried, Jeanne's son Marcel, now seven, died after suffering convulsions. Once more the death was ascribed to diphtheria, but doctors could not explain the marks around his neck. In less than a month, four Weber children had died. In each case, they had been left alone with Jeanne Weber and on every occasion she had been found holding the dead child in a state of evident excitement, but still no one suspected that she might be to blame.

On 5 April, the wife of Charles Weber arrived from Charenton, together with her 11-month-old son Maurice. Jeanne had lunch with her and Blanche at Pierre's house and afterwards Jeanne sent her sisters-in-law out on errands, leaving her alone with Maurice. However, the child's mother returned prematurely to find Jeanne hugging the child to her, suffocating him. Wresting him from her arms, Madame Charles Weber yelled: 'You wretch! You have strangled my son!'

She rushed him to Bretonneau Hospital, where doctors revived him, and after a night of intensive care Maurice recovered. A medical student then noticed the marks around his neck and concluded that an attempt had been made to strangle the child.

Acquitted of murder

On 8 April 1905, Charles Weber and his wife filed a complaint accusing Jeanne Weber of the attempted murder of their son Maurice. Pierre Weber followed them with a complaint about the suspicious deaths of his daughters Suzanne and Georgette, also reporting his suspicions about the deaths of his niece and nephew, Juliette and Marcel Weber. Then Léon Weber and his wife made a complaint about the death of

Germaine. The deaths of Lucie Alexandre and Marcelle Poyata also featured in the investigation.

Jeanne Weber was called in for questioning but she denied everything and claimed to be the victim of 'slanderers and infamous rascals'. She was pregnant at the time and miscarried while being held in Saint-Lazare Women's Prison.

Leading forensic scientist Dr Léon Thoinot was called in to examine Maurice and the exhumed bodies of the other Weber children but he was unable to confirm that any of them had been strangled. Nevertheless, the rumour spread that Jeanne Weber was a child strangler and she was charged with murder.

Her nine-day trial began on 29 January 1906 at the Cour d'assises de la Seine under Judge Bertulus, which was besieged by angry parents. Jeanne was defended by renowned lawyer Henri-Robert and played the role of a grieving mother. The prosecution had an impressive array of witnesses who testified that the accused had been alone with each of the children when they died. It was also alleged that she had killed her own son Marcel after the deaths of the other Weber children, to divert suspicion.

However, Dr Thoinot swung the jury in Jeanne's favour by saying: 'Science cannot tell you how these children came to die, but everything points to a natural death and that the accused is innocent.' Other expert witnesses testified that there was no conclusive proof that the children had been strangled and the jury then acquitted her, amid the outrage of those in court.

Madame Charles Weber cried 'There is no justice!', while Alphonse Alexandre stood on his seat and yelled: 'She will begin again!'

Jean Weber leapt over the benches to embrace his wife.

'I didn't kill them,' she said. 'Say that you believe me now.'

Differing views

The press were split on the question of her guilt. Noted journalist Michel Durand wrote:

> In the future let no one forget the fate of Jeanne Weber, the fate of an innocent woman, would have been sealed had she not lived in our age and in a Paris which is one of the greatest, if not the greatest, cradles of the exact science of forensic medicine. Science alone has won a victory for innocence and a triumph for itself; for the superiority of scientific knowledge over the testimony of witnesses and the detective work of the police has now been demonstrated.

Le Matin even organized fund-raisers for Jean and Jeanne, who were forced to move out of the Goutte d'Or by hostile neighbours and went to live in a hotel in Boulevard de la Chapelle. On 10 November 1906, a woman who claimed to have been robbed and thrown into the Seine was fished from the river. She gave her name as Jeanne Moulinet, Weber's maiden name. There was another failed suicide attempt on 30 December when she jumped off the bridge at Bercy. But air trapped under her skirt and petticoats kept her afloat until she was pulled from the icy water.

Deadly live-in housekeeper

The story of '*L'Ogresse de la Goutte d'Or*' had been followed by newspapers across France. Farmer Sylvain Bavouzet, a widower in Chambon in the province of Indre, had read it and was convinced of Jeanne Weber's innocence. He then wrote to her, inviting her to come and be his housekeeper. Jean did not fancy starting a new life in the provinces so Jeanne went alone, arriving on 13 March 1907. She took the name Jeanne Glaize and was introduced as the cousin of the late Madame Bavouzet, though she quickly became Bavouzet's mistress.

As well as cooking and cleaning, Jeanne's duties included looking after Bavouzet's children – 16-year-old Germaine, 11-year-old Louise and nine-year-old Auguste, who was said to be full of life. However, on 17 April 1907 he was a little under the weather when he came home from school. The following morning, Bavouzet went to fetch some milk while his two daughters played outside, leaving Jeanne alone with Auguste. When Bavouzet returned, Auguste was dead.

The local physician, Dr Papazoglou, was called. He found the boy's body scrubbed and cleaned and in his best clothes, with the collar buttoned tightly up around his neck.

'Why did you do that?' Dr Papazoglou asked.

'He vomited; he was dirty,' replied the housekeeper.

Dr Papazoglou then noticed the marks around Auguste's neck and refused to sign the death certificate. Instead, he went to the police, who assigned another doctor to the case. After examining the body Dr Charles Audiat then signed the certificate, declaring that Auguste Bavouzet had died of convulsions. The child was buried without any further explanation.

Walks free once again

Germaine Bavouzet was resentful that Jeanne had taken the place of her dead mother in her father's bed, but her papa had sworn the two girls to secrecy. Nevertheless, Germaine confirmed that their new housekeeper was indeed Weber when she found cuttings about the trial in the housekeeper's bag, which contained photographs showing the *Ogresse*. Fearing that she or her younger sister might be her next victims, she took the cuttings to the police.

While the local gendarmes discreetly investigated the case, *Le Matin* got wind of it and sent a journalist to interview Jeanne. Auguste's body was exhumed and bruises and strangulation marks were found around his neck. Meanwhile, the Poyata family and Paul Alexandre, the uncle of little Lucie, filed fresh complaints.

Weber was arrested and incarcerated. Henri-Robert rallied to her defence again and called in Dr Thoinot. He examined the body and questioned the abilities of Dr Bruneau, the provincial physician who had performed the autopsy. Auguste had died of typhoid fever, Thoinot proclaimed. A dispute about the cause of death raged in the academic journals and a third post-mortem was ordered. This proved inconclusive and once again Jeanne Weber walked free.

'Jeanne is free,' wrote one provincial newspaper indignantly, 'and so are Thoinot and Robert.'

Many supporters

Henri-Robert revelled in his victory, telling the Paris Society of Forensic Medicine that Dr Bruneau was an ignorant and inept doctor, while lauding Thoinot.

'After eight months of pre-trial imprisonment, Jeanne Weber was released,' he said. 'You now know who bears responsibility for that imprisonment.'

This damaged Dr Bruneau's career and standing.

Despite the death of one more child in her charge, Weber still had many supporters. She was then seen working as an orderly in a children's hospital in Faucombault, but did not stay there long because of her growing alcoholism. However, George Bonjean, president for the Society for the Protection of Children, gave her a job in a children's home in Orgeville to 'make up for the wrongs that justice has inflicted upon an innocent woman'. She worked there under the name of Marie Lemoine, but a few days after she was hired she was caught with her hands around the neck of a sick child. She was fired, but to maintain the reputation of the institution Bonjean kept quiet about the incident.

Confesses to police

On her return to Paris, Weber was arrested as a vagrant and confessed to the police: 'I am the woman who killed the children in the Goutte d'Or.' However, when she was brought before the Prefect of Police she denied it, so he sent her to the mental asylum in Nanterre, where she was found to be sane and then released. She repeated her confession in

Alfortville and narrowly escaped being lynched by a mob. Once more she admitted that she was a murderer to the police who rallied to her protection, but they dismissed her confession as drunken ravings.

She then became the mistress of a man named Joly and lived with him in his lodgings near Toul. Then she turned to prostitution, servicing the railway workers in Bar-le-Duc. She moved to Commercy with one of them, Emile Boucheri, and he and one Jeanne Moulinet took a room in an inn run by a family named Poirot, where Jeanne helped out by looking after the Poirots' six-year-old son Marcel.

On 8 March 1908, Weber told Madame Poirot that her common-law husband was a jealous brute who beat her when he came home drunk and asked if she would let her six-year-old son Marcel sleep with her. That way she would escape a beating.

Caught red-handed

In the night, another guest named Madame Curlet heard loud noises from Weber's room and went to alert the owners. When a knock on the door of Jeanne Moulinet's door garnered no response, Monsieur Poirot opened it with a pass key to discover Weber straddling his son. There was a handkerchief around the boy's neck and blood was flowing from his mouth. Poirot had to hit Weber three times in the face to get her to release her grip on the boy's throat, but Marcel was already dead.

Jeanne was arrested but remained silent. A post-mortem found that she had bitten off the boy's tongue and strangled him with a wet handkerchief. This time there was no doubt that the child had been murdered so there was nothing Henri-Robert or Dr Thoinot could do to save her.

Declared insane

On 25 August 1908 Jeanne Weber was declared insane and locked up in a hospital in Maréville, still protesting her innocence. The public fumed with indignation at the doctors who had allowed the child killer to escape justice and roam free to kill again and meanwhile Jean Weber filed for divorce.

Jeanne Weber was transferred to an asylum at Fains-Véel in Meuse. On 22 April 1909 a rumour spread through La Chapelle that the *Ogresse* had escaped. A woman who looked like her was surrounded by an angry mob and Jean Weber had to be called to confirm that she was not his wife. Then in August there was another panic that she had escaped. *Le Matin* showed no further interest in Jeanne Weber, but *Le Petit Journal* sent a journalist to the asylum where he found her hospitalized and bedridden.

However, in January 1910 she did escape in truth, but she was only free for a few weeks. She was arrested on 10 February at Châtelier in the Meuse, while she was trying to get a job on a farm in the village.

Weber died on 23 August 1918 during a 'crisis of madness'. A wail of horror came from her cell and when doctors arrived they found she had ripped out her throat with her own nails.

MARTHA RENDELL

Martha Rendell was the common-law wife of Thomas Morris. In 1909 she was hanged for the cold-blooded murder of three of his children by swabbing their throats with spirits of salts – otherwise known as hydrochloric acid. This inflamed their throats so that they could no longer eat. The children suffered slow and agonizing deaths, enduring stomach pains, vomiting, diarrhoea and fits before they finally succumbed.

The deaths of Annie, aged nine, and Olive, aged seven, were attributed to diphtheria – there had been an outbreak of the disease in Western Australia in 1907. But when 15-year-old Arthur died, the doctor requested a post mortem. Martha Rendell stood in on the autopsy but nothing untoward was found.

Hydrochloric acid

In early April 1909, Thomas Morris's second son George went missing. When the police found him, he said that he had run away because his stepmother was trying to poison him – as she had his brother and two sisters.

It was discovered that Rendell had obtained large quantities of spirits of salts during the period of the children's illnesses, but none since the last death. A neighbour said she had seen Rendell swabbing

Arthur Morris's throat and had heard his agonized screams and cries for help. The bottle gave off strong, acrid fumes that produced a burning sensation, but Rendell claimed a doctor had prescribed the medication.

Doctors were unsure what effect swabbing with hydrochloric acid would have. The Department of Health experimented on rabbits and guinea pigs and demonstrated that such swabbing caused similar effects as those seen in the children. The children's bodies were exhumed and traces of hydrochloric acid were found. It had caused inflammation and haemorrhage of the bowel.

Both Thomas Morris and Martha Rendell were charged with murder. Morris was acquitted, even though he was the one who had purchased the spirits of salts. Rendell protested her innocence, saying she was only treating the children for diphtheria.

Throughout the hearing she wore black with her face covered by a heavy black veil. 'It could be seen, however, that frequently during the hearing of the evidence she smiled in an amused and scornful manner at parts, which, to the other listeners in court, were fraught with the most sinister suggestions and hideous horror,' according to the *Truth* of 14 August 1909.

No motive

Although no motive could be found for the murders, Rendell was found guilty and sentenced to death. To the end, Thomas Morris stood by her. He told the *West Australian*: 'I know her better than anyone else, and I say she was incapable of doing what is attributed to her. She may have appeared hard outwardly, but no woman had a more tender heart than she.'

Walking unassisted to the gallows, Rendell said: 'I am completely and absolutely innocent of the crimes for which I am dying.' Rendell was hanged in Fremantle Prison at 8 a.m. on 6 October 1909. At no stage did she show any remorse. She was the last woman to be hanged in Western Australia.

HENRY CLARK AND AUGUSTA FULHAM

ndia is infested with poisonous snakes, none more deadly than the human variety. Some blame the stifling heat, others the exotic setting for the strange effect the subcontinent had on its white colonial inhabitants in the days of the Raj. Many prim upper-class ladies and starch-collared gentlemen lost their inhibitions when the sun went down. One fatally affected fellow was Dr Henry Clark, who blamed the murder of his wife on the 'thugees', a fanatical cult who worshipped Kali, the eight-armed goddess of death. Dr Clark had a cast-iron alibi, which placed him several miles away at the time of the killing in March 1913 and in full view of several reliable witnesses. While the investigation cleared Clark of the murder of his wife, it uncovered a series of nefarious deeds.

There were rumours that the good doctor had been guilty of conduct unbecoming a gentleman as he had pursued a relationship with a married woman, Mrs Augusta Fulham. These rumours proved to be well founded – the police found almost 400 letters from Dr Clark to Mrs Fulham when they searched the lady's home in Agra. The letters did not only contain words of love – they also revealed the details of a plot to poison the unsuspecting Mr Fulham. Dr Clark supplied the arsenic powder and Augusta administered it. When her husband complained of stomach cramps he was taken to hospital, where Dr Clark finished him off with a second dose. The thugees, it transpired, had been paid by Dr Clark to remove his wife from the scene so that he could be comforted in his bereavement by the young widow. The couple would then arouse little suspicion when they married. Sadly, the only solemn vows Dr Clark made were to the priest who accompanied him to the gallows on 26 March 1913. Fulham was spared the noose because she was pregnant at the time of her trial, but she was given a life sentence in one of India's most formidable prisons. Mercifully, she died of heatstroke the following year.

AMY ARCHER-GILLIGAN

Amy Archer-Gilligan was a widow in her 40s when she stood trial for murder in 1917. She then lived out her days in a hospital for the criminally insane. The case was unlikely material for comedy. However, New York playwright Joseph Kesselring remembered reading about it when he was a boy and 20 years later he went to Connecticut to examine newspaper accounts and records. The result was the play *Arsenic and Old Lace*, which opened on Broadway in 1941 and ran for three and a half years. Veteran movie director Frank Capra then turned the play into a classic movie of the same name, starring Cary Grant.

Mrs Archer-Gilligan was born Amy Duggan in Milton, Connecticut, in 1868, the eighth of ten children. There was mental illness in the family because her brother John became an inmate of the Connecticut General Hospital for the Insane in 1902 and he was later joined by one of her sisters.

Care home opened

In 1897, Amy married James Archer and the couple had a baby daughter named Mary. Four years later, they moved to Newington, Connecticut, to work as carers for elderly widower John Seymour, in exchange for room and board. When Seymour died in 1904, the Archers rented the house from his heirs and turned it into Sister Amy's Nursing Home for the Elderly.

Seymour's family decided to sell the house in 1906 and the Archers moved on to Windsor, Connecticut, where they used their savings to buy a brick-built house at 37 Prospect Street. This became the Archer Home for Elderly and Indigent Persons. They advertised in local newspapers and handed out flyers to find clients, or 'inmates' as they called them. Lodgers could pay a weekly fee of $7 to $25, or a flat fee of $1,000 (worth over £18,000/$24,000 now) for lifetime care. Many chose the latter option.

As care for the elderly outside the family was relatively new, there was little regulation of care homes. However, in 1909 the McClintock family of West Hartford sued the Archers for their poor treatment of an elderly family member. The case was settled out of court, with the Archers paying $5,000.

Death of husbands

In 1910, James Archer died of Bright's disease, a catch-all name for kidney failure of an unknown cause, leaving Amy with a 12-year-old daughter to bring up, which was not cheap. Mary had been enrolled in Windsor's Campbell School for Girls, where the fees were $410 a year (about £8,500/$11,000 now), plus $50 for piano lessons, as she was a budding musician. Amy also found herself liable for back taxes and wrote to Windsor tax collector Howard L. Goslee, saying:

> I ask to be dealt with honestly – that is all – I fully realize my great loss and sorrow and that I am alone dependent upon myself to care and educate my little daughter who was deprived of her dear father whom she loved so dearly. But I am not afraid to demand justice, and I think it is about time that it is shown me.

In 1913, Mrs Archer married again. Her new husband was 56-year-old Michael Gilligan, but the marriage lasted just three months, as Gilligan suddenly died.

The death certificate listed 'valvular heart disease' as the primary cause of death, with a secondary cause given as 'acute bilious attack' – that is, very bad indigestion. He left her $4,000.

Flat fee residents died soonest

While many of the inmates of the Archer Home could not be expected to live long, 61-year-old Franklin R. Andrews was surprisingly fit and healthy. He did gardening and work around the house and ran errands for Mrs Archer-Gilligan. Andrews often wrote to his sister, Nellie Pierce, mentioning the frequent deaths at the care home. The mortality rate was particularly high among those who paid the flat fee. Those who paid weekly could expect to live longer.

On the morning of 29 May 1914 Mr Andrews was seen painting a fence on the property, but at 11 p.m. that night Mrs Archer-Gilligan phoned his sister, telling her that he was ill. However, she said it would not be necessary to visit until the following morning. When Mr Andrews's sister arrived the next day, she was told that her brother had died in the night. The cause of death was given as gastric ulcers. His sister grew suspicious about his death when she went through her dead brother's papers and discovered that Mrs Archer-Gilligan had been badgering him for money. She went to the district attorney, who showed no interest, so she approached the local newspaper, *The Hartford Courant*.

High mortality rate

The *Courant*'s correspondent in Windsor, Carlan Goslee, wrote the obituaries of the town's residents and had long been troubled by the death rate at the Archer Home. He visited the local drugstore, H.H. Mason's on Broad Street Green, and examined the poisons register that every drugstore was obliged to keep. There he discovered that

Mrs Archer-Gilligan often bought arsenic, saying she used it to kill rats and bedbugs.

Courant editor Clifford Sherman then opened a full investigation. Reporters went through the death certificates and found there had been 60 deaths in the Archer Home between 1907 and 1916 – 12 before 1911 and 48 from 1911 to 1916, after Mrs Archer-Gilligan had got into financial difficulties. This was a shockingly high mortality rate, as only ten or 12 people lived at the home at any one time. The Jefferson Street Home in nearby Hartford had a similar number of deaths but had seven times as many inmates.

Residents at the Archer Home frequently died suddenly and the death certificate often cited a stomach problem. It was then discovered that just before Michael Gilligan's death Mrs Archer-Gilligan had bought 283 g (10 oz) of arsenic – enough to kill 100 people. Reporters also found that she had been buying morphine.

The state police then began to take an interest. On 2 May 1916, Mr Andrews's body was exhumed and his stomach was found to contain enough arsenic 'to kill half-a-dozen strong men'. This led to other bodies being dug up too – including that of Mr Gilligan.

Money taken from deceased

A week later, the state police went to the Archer Home to ask Mrs Archer-Gilligan about the deaths of her inmates. She said: 'Well, we didn't ask them to come here but we do the best we can for them. They are old people, and some live for a long time while others die after being here a short time.'

Questioned about the financial arrangements she made with the deceased, she said she barely scraped by: 'I am a poor, hard-working woman and I can't understand why I am persecuted as I have been during the last few years. This is a Christian work and one that is very trying as we have to put up with lots of things on account of the peculiarities of the old people.'

On 8 May 1917 she was arrested for murder. She protested, saying: 'I will prove my innocence, if it takes my last mill. I am not guilty and I will hang before they prove it.'

The following day, the front page of the *Hartford Courant* carried the headline: 'POLICE BELIEVE ARCHER HOME FOR AGED A MURDER FACTORY.'

The story under it read:

> The arrest of the Windsor woman yesterday is the result of the suspicions aroused when Mrs Nellie E. Pierce of No. 205 Vine St., Hartford, found in the effects of her brother, Franklin R. Andrews, after he died at the Archer House, a letter from Mrs Archer-Gilligan asking for a loan, 'as near $1,000 as possible,' about which the woman had said nothing to her.

When Mrs Pierce asked Mrs Archer-Gilligan about the loan, she denied receiving one at first. Later, she said she had received $500 as a gift. After Mrs Pierce had hired a lawyer to demand the return of the money, Archer-Gilligan paid it back, 'not because she could not keep it but because she did not feel it worth quarreling over,' the *Courant* reported.

Statement of the accused

From Hartford County Jail, Archer-Gilligan issued a long statement, saying:

> Shortly after Mr Andrews's death, I received information that the authorities were trying to connect his death with some criminal act on the part of somebody in the home. Some of the neighbours in Windsor distorted the facts and invented stories to keep the agitation alive.
>
> Some of the inmates of the home told me from time to time that they were told they were liable to be poisoned if

they remained in the home, and one old gentleman, over 90 years of age and ailing, went so far as to intimate that a glass of lemonade served to him when he was suffering from a severe cold had been drugged. The physician in attendance on him at the time was requested to make an analysis of the lemonade and did so by drinking it in the presence of the old gentleman who suspected it was drugged. The man still lives.

For a period of several months I was constantly informed that the authorities had examined the conduct of the home, but, knowing that I had done no wrong and that there was nothing that I should fear as a result of the investigation, I continued to manage the home and solicited patronage.

Many of the inmates die, which is not strange, because they were sent to the Home when they were either too old or too feeble to care for themselves and at a time when their relatives considered them such a burden that they had to be cared for by some institution. Most of them were ailing from diseases other than those which usually accompany advanced age. In each instance, when a death occurred the relatives were notified, unless, perchance, the relatives had left word not to be notified, in other words, had abandoned the inmate.

I have had hundreds of aged, helpless and infirm and have ministered to their wants and given them such comforts as the Home could afford, and I think they were all satisfied with the treatment received. When I was arrested, I asked the police officers if it would not be better for me to consult an attorney, and they told me to follow their advice, that they were friendly to me and wanted to carry the thing through without notoriety. I followed their advice, and now I am in jail without a hearing.

The public knows nothing of my side of the case, nothing about the real facts behind my arrest and imprisonment. After I was locked up here in jail Captain Hurley of the State Police came to me, again advised me as a friend, and told me that they had four charges of murder against me. If I was to sign a statement, he said, admitting one charge, they would drop the other three. Thank God I did not follow his advice because my counsel informs me that if I had this so-called friend would have rounded out his friendly advice with a conviction on the awful crime of murder, and I am innocent of wrongdoing against any person who had ever been an inmate of my house, in either thought, word, or deed, as any child of 5 years.

I am told it is claimed that I took persons under a life contract and tried to make a profit by poisoning them. An examination of the records, which have been seized by the State Police, will show the absurdity of such a statement. I have conducted this home for years. I inherited a little property from my parents, and when my husband, Mr Gilligan, died he left a will, leaving his property to someone other than myself. I am today in jail, charged with murder, knowing nothing of the evidence against me nor whom it is that I am charged with having murdered.

I have two small pieces of real estate, worth from $8,000 to $9,000, mortgaged for $4,750, and I have worked all my life, cooking and scrubbing and washing, giving personal attention to the home and trying to educate my 18-year-old daughter, who is heartbroken because of the charge which has been brought against me.

When she was here at the jail this morning it almost broke my heart to learn that a picture of my baby had been put on the front page of a Hartford newspaper. This was a cowardly outrage, and I hope the man responsible for it will some day feel a little anguish and agony which a mother's heart feels now as a result of his mean and contemptible conduct.

When I was managing the home I contracted small bills, and my lawyer tells me today that a kind-hearted Deputy Sheriff in

Windsor has placed attachments upon the little bit of property I had, making it impossible for me to further mortgage and so raise funds for my defense. It seems as if all the world has turned against me, and at times I feel a forlorn and defenseless woman, but I try to have faith in God, and my love for my baby girl will give me strength to live until my innocence is proved. I want a chance to prove my innocence.

This statement was reprinted in *The New York Times* under the headline: 'MRS GILLIGAN SAYS SHE IS PERSECUTED.'

Arsenic found in corpses

The newspaper went on to report that the State Bacteriologist, Dr A.J. Wolff, said enough poison had been found in Mr Andrews's body to kill several people. The embalmer, Frank P. Smith of Hartford, said he did not know if arsenic had been used in the preparation of the embalming fluid.

'The fluid came from New York,' he said. 'I don't know the formula.'

Another of the bodies to be exhumed was that of Mrs Alice Gowdy, who had died at the age of 69. She and her 71-year-old husband, Loren B. Gowdy, had enquired about moving into the Archer Home in May 1914. They wanted to move into the room occupied by Mr Andrews on 1 June and he died conveniently on 30 May. The Gowdys got a telegram the following day, saying they could move in after they had stumped up the fixed fee of $1,000. Mrs Gowdy died on 4 December 1914 and when her body was exhumed it showed traces of arsenic. However, Mr Gowdy survived long enough to testify at Archer-Gilligan's trial over two years later.

Life sentence

While the authorities thought Mrs Archer-Gilligan had killed at least 20 residents, she was indicted for the murders of five people: Franklin

Andrews, Alice Gowdy, Michael Gilligan, Charles A. Smith who died on 9 April 1914 and Maud Howard Lynch who died on 2 February 1916. All but Lynch had died of arsenic poisoning – she had been poisoned with strychnine. However, Mrs Archer-Gilligan was eventually tried for only one murder, that of Mr Andrews.

The trial began on 21 June 1917 in Hartford. It drew large crowds and was covered widely in the press. Mrs Archer-Gilligan was convicted and sentenced to death by hanging, but the conviction was overturned on a technicality and a retrial was ordered. At the second trial in June 1919 she changed her plea to not guilty on the grounds of insanity. A forensic psychiatrist then confirmed she was crazy, while her daughter Mary testified that her mother was a morphine addict. The trial ended abruptly when Mrs Archer-Gilligan changed her plea again, this time to guilty of second-degree murder. This brought a life sentence.

Arsenic and Old Lace

She began her sentence at the state prison in Wethersfield, but five years later she was certified insane and transferred to the Connecticut General Hospital for the Insane at Middletown. There she was described as a quiet and co-operative patient. When she died in 1962 at the age of 94, the *Courant* reported: 'Mostly she sat in a chair, dressed in a black dress trimmed with lace, a Bible on her lap, and prayed.'

In the play and film *Arsenic and Old Lace*, the 'Connecticut Borgia' was transformed into two sisters, maiden aunts living in Brooklyn. Their victims were aged men who lived in their boarding house and the old-fashioned murder weapon of choice was elderberry wine spiked with arsenic. The cast of characters included a dotty brother, Teddy – who thought he was Teddy Roosevelt at San Juan Hill and was forever yelling 'CHARGE!' and running up the stairs – and two nephews, the sane Mortimer and the homicidal Jonathan.

The Duggan family continued to live in the village of Milton in Connecticut. One of Amy's brothers would stand in front of a mirror all day, playing the violin. He shared a house on Saw Mill Road with a sister who became an invalid after jumping or falling from a second-floor window.

Doubts about guilt

There are some who doubt that Amy Archer-Gilligan was guilty. The Windsor Historical Society maintains a file on Amy Archer-Gilligan and when Ruth Bonito from the Historical Society of nearby Windsor Locks checked it out she concluded that Amy may have been innocent. She never confessed to the crimes and the evidence against her was purely circumstantial. Although she bought arsenic, she may well have used it to kill rats and bedbugs, as she said. The Archer Home did have a high mortality rate, but that did not prove that she poisoned the inmates – or that they were poisoned at all.

True, arsenic was found in the bodies that had been exhumed. However, arsenic was once used extensively by American embalmers, a fact confirmed in 1997 by Connecticut's state archaeologist, Nicholas Bellantoni. In 1908, Connecticut's legislature banned embalming fluids containing arsenic because its use made it impossible for forensic scientists to ascertain whether residues in bodies were the result of poisoning or embalming. Formaldehyde-based embalming fluids were to be used instead, but these gave off toxic fumes and could only be used in places where there was proper ventilation. Consequently, some undertakers continued using arsenic-based fluids illegally. At the very least, this could have been a key argument for the defence.

Mrs Bonito also pointed out that Amy Archer-Gilligan was a churchgoing woman who donated a stained-glass window to St Gabriel's Church in Windsor. This hardly made her the type of woman who would turn to serial killing in middle age.

MARIE ALEXANDRINE BECKER

iège housewife Marie Alexandrine Becker lived a blameless life until she was 55. Then she began a spree of murder, theft and forgery. The profits she made from her crimes were squandered on a series of young lovers.

Her crimes came to light when an old woman died of 'acute indigestion'. There was nothing immediately suspicious about her death and a doctor and a nurse were present. However, a complaint had been made on a report that passed across the desk of the Police Commissioner, Honore Lebrun, on 3 October 1935. He was immediately struck by the name of the deceased's nurse, Marie Becker. Her name had appeared on two other recent reports of women who had died from 'acute indigestion'. Was this just a coincidence? He set up an investigation.

Mrs Becker had been born Marie Alexandrine Petitjean to a family of poor farm workers in Wamont, in the Flemish-speaking region of Belgium, in 1877. An ambitious woman, she wanted more out of life than toiling on a farm. A local priest taught her reading, writing and arithmetic and at 16 she left home to take up an apprenticeship in dressmaking in Liège.

Lavished gifts on lovers

While still young, she married Charles Becker, who owned a sawmill. Later he invested in a furniture factory. Marie used her dressmaking skills to copy the latest fashions from Paris but she craved more. She had a series of young lovers and took up with middle-aged rake Lambert Beyer, who made her acquaintance when she was buying vegetables at a market stall. Her staid and reliable husband stood in the way of this tempestuous romance but in 1932 he died of 'acute indigestion'. She collected on his life insurance and invested the money in a dress shop. But she soon tired of Beyer and he died too, leaving her more money.

Becker was then seen dancing wildly with men at the local nightclubs, outraging the respectable ladies of Liège. Often she would pay young gigolos to escort her home and take her to bed. Her particular favourite was the handsome Maximilian Houdy, 20 years her junior, on whom she lavished expensive gifts. But the business failed and soon she was short of money.

First brush with the law

One day in March 1933, she went to the cinema with Marie Doupagne-Castaldot, who agreed to loan her 19,000 Belgian francs. Afterwards, they went for a drink together. Doupagne-Castaldot then fell ill and Becker offered to look after her, but under Becker's care her symptoms soon grew worse and she died. An anonymous letter was sent to the prosecutor's office, which prompted a report that ended up on the Commissioner's desk, and Becker was arrested. She had apparently nursed a number of other elderly friends who suffered a similar fate.

'It seems that those who entrust themselves to your care have an undeviating tendency to die suddenly,' the investigating magistrate declared.

'But they are old,' Becker replied. 'What would you have? Is it not that everyone dies so, sooner or later?'

'That is true,' said the magistrate. 'But also it is possible for the old to die before their time. I understand that you invariably served your patients tea, and justice demands that you inform me what you put into the tea.'

'Herbs,' said Becker. 'Only herbs of the most beneficent kinds. Herbs that would have healed them if it was that they were to live.'

String of murders

However, there was no direct evidence to support a charge of murder and Becker was released. Instead of regarding this brush with the law as a warning, Becker continued working for rich, elderly women whose mortality rate was suspiciously high. It was later discovered that if she did not acquire money by directly stealing from her victims she got it by forging their wills or otherwise obtaining money by fraud.

When she ran out of elderly friends, she turned to the customers of the boutique she had invested in. Victims would be invited into a back room of the shop to discuss the latest fashions and she would offer them a cup of tea or a glass of wine. She would then accompany them home, where she took over as nurse, with the same results as before.

One such was Marie-Louise Evrard-Crulle, who died on 11 November 1935. Relatives noted to their astonishment that she had left her money to a young man who was completely unknown to them. It turned out that the heir was a close friend of Marie Becker. A second anonymous letter then turned up at the prosecutor's office, accusing Becker of murder and the misappropriation of the inheritance. Although doctors ascribed the death to hepatic colic, which had triggered a heart attack, Becker remained under surveillance.

More evidence accrued and then her friend, Madame Guichner, contacted the police. Guichner said she had complained to Becker about her husband, saying: 'I wish he were dead.' Becker then replied:

'If you really mean that, I can supply you with a powder that will leave no trace.' She disposed of ten to 12 old ladies this way and even attended their funerals, where she was seen dressed in black and kneeling at the graveside in tears. After leaving the cemetery, she would scurry off to spend their money on young men.

Marie Becker.

Caught in the act

On 30 September 1936, she went to the funeral of Madame Lange with Madame Weiss and Madame Lamy, inviting them to her home afterwards. Madame Weiss died a few hours later. The police then asked Madame Lamy to invite Becker round to her house. When Becker arrived, she was arrested and the police found a bottle of digitalis in her handbag.

'I suffered from heart trouble,' she explained, 'and I had to take it. I did not want my lover to know.'

In small doses, digitalis is used to cure cardiac arrhythmia, but an overdose can kill, producing symptoms like those of acute indigestion. When doctors examined Madame Becker they could find nothing wrong with her heart. As the judge later put it: 'In spite of your heart trouble you were known to go to dance halls and behave like a strong and flirtatious young woman. The druggist and chemist you name are dead, but the police have found no entries of your case in their registers.'

When the police visited Becker and searched her home, they found clothing, jewellery and other items belonging to her victims, along with a bag Madame Weiss had used to keep 40,000 Belgian francs in. Meanwhile, a panel of experts had to study the effects of digitalis to prove it was a credible murder weapon.

Found guilty of murder

Becker spent 17 months in prison, while the bodies of her victims were exhumed. Traces of digitalis were found in all of them. The indictment was 12,000 words long and took the court clerk three hours to read out. In the packed courtroom Becker was faced with ten lawyers, 1,800 items of evidence and 294 witnesses, every one of whose statements she contested.

'Everyone in the case is lying except you?' asked the judge.

'Yes,' she replied, nodding vigorously.

Throughout she maintained the pose of an innocent woman who had been wronged by these accusations. She kept asking the judge to hurry as she had other matters to attend to but his response was that she had yet to clear herself.

One explanation of Becker's middle-aged murder spree is that she was trying to recapture her lost youth. It was reported that she appeared in court made up gaudily and dressed like a 16-year-old flapper. A dozen former teenage lovers testified that she had lavished money and presents on them and she was forced to admit that this left her always in need of money. In her defence, she said: 'As for my going out with young people, my theory has always been that one is as young as one thinks oneself to be. As for what little money I spent on my friends from time to time, well, somehow Providence always saw to it that I was well cared for in worldly things. I seldom worried.'

Distraught as Becker had seemed at the funerals of her victims, in the dock she gloated over her crimes. She said one victim, Madame Lambert, 'looked like an angel choked with sauerkraut', while she saw Madame Doupagne-Castaldot 'dying beautifully, lying flat on her back'.

Marie Alexandrine Becker was found guilty of 11 murders and sentenced to death. However, in Belgium the death sentence is automatically commuted to life imprisonment. She died in jail in 1942, aged 61.

ANNA MARIE HAHN

The press dubbed Anna Marie Hahn 'The Blonde Borgia' after the Renaissance femme fatale Lucrezia Borgia, famed for poisoning dinner guests with lethal doses administered from a hollow ring – though there is no historic evidence that she did any such thing. Anna Marie Hahn certainly did though. At the age of 32, she was the first woman to die in the electric chair in Ohio. She had been sentenced to death for the murder of 78-year-old Jacob Wagner, though the prosecution linked her to the deaths of at least five elderly men, whom she also robbed, using a variety of poisons. In court, much attention was paid to her elegant attire and beautiful coiffure. However, she lost some of it when a patch was shaved to attach the electrode from Old Sparky in Ohio State Penitentiary.

Arrested on suspicion

Her crimes were discovered when another elderly man, 67-year-old George Obendorfer, died at the Memorial Hospital in Colorado Springs on 1 August 1937. The doctors could not ascertain a cause of death so the police were called in to investigate.

When he was taken ill, Obendorfer had been staying at the Park Hotel, whose owner had just filed a report concerning the theft of $300 worth of diamonds (some $5,000 now). According to the register, Obendorfer was from Cincinnati, Ohio, and had registered with Anna Hahn and her young son Oskar, also from Cincinnati. However, when their rooms were checked, there was no sign of her. Detectives discovered that a woman answering Hahn's description had been trying to pawn jewellery and withdraw $1,000 ($15,000 now) from a Denver bank using Obendorfer's bank book. She claimed to be Mrs Obendorfer, but detectives were convinced that she was Anna Hahn.

Once back in Cincinnati, she was arrested. At first, she claimed not to know Obendorfer but when she was reminded that she had checked in to the Park Hotel in Colorado Springs with him, she claimed that she had only met him on the train and was trying to help him. However, according to Obendorfer's family the couple had planned to travel to Colorado together to view a ranch she said she owned. During their interviews, the police looked further into her background.

Marriage

Born Anna Marie Filser in Bavaria in 1906, she had emigrated to the United States in 1929 with her husband, a Viennese doctor, and their son Oskar. Her husband died soon after they arrived in Cincinnati, but Anna decided to stay on. At a dance in the city's German district, she met Philip Hahn. They married and went into business running delicatessens. After a fire in one of their shops, Anna collected $300 from the insurance company. Two fires in their marital home netted a further $2,000 and the police began to suspect she was an arsonist.

Then she attempted to persuade her husband to take out life insurance for $25,000, but he refused. Nevertheless, Philip Hahn soon fell desperately ill and his mother took him to hospital against Anna's wishes. He survived the mysterious illness, but the couple separated shortly afterwards. Anna then supported herself by nursing elderly patients, though she had no previous experience in the field.

Deadly nurse

Detectives found that Anna Hahn had been nursing retired gardener Jacob Wagner, who had died mysteriously two months before Obendorfer, leaving his entire estate to Anna Hahn. They learned that she had claimed to be his long-lost niece, though he had no living relatives. Neighbours said that she spent hours in his apartment after his death. Not only that, but a lady in his block whom Hahn had

Anna Marie Hahn claimed she did not kill Wagner for his money and that forging his will was an afterthought.

befriended fell violently ill after eating an ice cream that Hahn had given her. While she was in hospital, money and jewellery was stolen from her apartment. And when Wagner's body was exhumed it was found to contain high levels of arsenic.

After seeing reports in the press, 62-year-old George Heis then came forward, saying that a year before he had fallen violently ill after Hahn, his carer, had poured a beer for him. He became suspicious when two houseflies that had sampled the brew dropped dead. When she refused a taste, he sacked her. Though he continued to suffer after-effects, he survived to testify against her.

Weeks before she travelled to Colorado, another of her patients, 77-year-old George Gsellman, had fallen ill and died. When his body was exhumed it was found to contain a large amount of croton oil – a diarrhoea medicine that can kill in large doses. Philip Hahn then handed over a bottle of croton oil that he had taken from his wife. A local pharmacist, who knew Anna personally, confirmed that she had bought it.

During a search of her home, the police found an IOU for $2,000. She had apparently borrowed money from 72-year-old Albert Palmer, who died while she was nursing him through a lengthy illness. After his death she had kept the money and taken back the note. According to relatives, a further $4,000 was missing from his estate.

When Anna's son Oskar was questioned, he contradicted his mother's story that they had met Obendorfer by chance on the train. Instead, she had bought his ticket in Union Terminal, Cincinnati. She had also given him several drinks on the train and he had begun to feel ill before they arrived in Colorado.

Charged with murder

There was a warrant for 'grand larceny' out for her in Colorado, in connection with the diamonds. However, instead of shipping her back there, the authorities in Ohio decided to charge her with the murder

83

of Jacob Wagner, using the other mysterious deaths as corroborating evidence.

In court, witnesses were called to give evidence about Wagner's agonizing end. A chemist testified that he had found enough arsenic in his body to kill four men and a handwriting expert said that Wagner's will was a forgery. The handwriting was Hahn's.

Hahn took the stand in her own defence. She denied the accusations, and could not be tripped up in cross-examination, but there was little she could do to contest the forensic evidence against her. The prosecutor, Dudley Outcalt, sealed her fate with his closing statement, saying:

> She is sly, because she developed her relationships with old men who had no relatives and lived alone. She is avaricious, because no act was so low but that she was ready to commit it for slight gain. She is cold-blooded, like no other woman in the world, because no one could sit here for four weeks and hear this damaging parade of evidence and display no emotion. She is heartless, because nobody with a heart could deal out the death she dealt these old men. We've seen here the coldest, most heartless cruel person that ever has come within the scope of our lives. In the four corners of this courtroom stand four dead men. Gsellman, Palmer, Wagner, Obendorfer! From the four corners bony fingers point at her and say: 'That woman poisoned me! That woman made my last moments an agony! That woman tortured me with the tortures of the damned!' Then, turning to you they say: 'Let my death be not entirely in vain. My life cannot be brought back, but through my death and the punishment to be inflicted upon her, you can prevent such a death from coming to another man.' From the four corners of this room, those old men say to you, 'Do your duty!' I ask of you, for the state of Ohio, that you withhold any recommendations of mercy.

The attorney for the defence, Joseph H. Hoodin, had little to counter this.

> I will not say that a single witness lied, but this case has had such widespread publicity that it would have been impossible for these witnesses not to have preconceived ideas before they ever came into this courtroom. Particularly this is true of the witnesses from Wagner's neighbourhood, where the case has been the chief topic of conversation for months. Although she is no angel, she is not guilty of the murder of Jacob Wagner.

Sentenced to death

The jury of 11 women and one man were not convinced by this. They took just two hours to return a verdict of guilty, with no recommendation for mercy. This meant an automatic sentence of death. Before formally sentencing her on 10 November 1937, Judge Charles S. Bell asked Hahn if she had anything to say.

'I have,' she replied. 'I am innocent, your honour.'

Judge Bell then said:

> It is ordered, adjudged, and desired by the court that the defendant, Anna Marie Hahn, be taken hence to jail in Hamilton County, Ohio, and that within 30 days hereof the Sheriff of Hamilton County shall convey the said defendant to the Ohio penitentiary and deliver her to the warden thereof, and that on the tenth day of March, 1938 the said warden shall cause a current of electricity sufficient to cause death to pass through the body of the said defendant, the application of such current to be continued until the said defendant is dead.

Then he turned to Hahn and said: 'And may God, in his infinite wisdom, have mercy on your soul.'

Appeals went all the way up to the US Supreme Court, to no avail. On 6 December 1938, it was announced that the execution would take place at 8 p.m. the following day. In the time left to her, Hahn wrote four letters which she handed to her attorney. One contained her confession, which was sold to the *Cincinnati Enquirer*. The money was put in trust for Oskar's education.

Confession

I don't know how I could have done the things I did in my life. Only God knows what came over me when I gave Albert Palmer, that first one, that poison that caused his death. Up in heaven there is a God who will judge. He will know and He will tell me how it came about. He will tell me what caused me to do the same things to Mr Wagner and the last one, Mr Obendorfer. I never knew myself afterwards, and I don't know now.

When those poor men were sick I tried to do everything for them. When I stood by Mr Wagner as he was laid out at the funeral home I don't know how it was I didn't scream out at the top of my voice. I couldn't in my mind believe that it was me, Anna Marie Hahn, who loved people so well and wanted friends all the time, that could have put Mr Wagner there. I can't believe it even today. I couldn't believe it when in the court those people came to the room and told the jury how they said these men died. I was sitting there hearing a story like out of a book all about another person.

As things come to my mind now and as I put them on this paper I can't believe I am writing about things I did myself. However, they must be about me because they are in my mind and I know them. God above will tell me what made me do these terrible things. I couldn't have been in my right mind when I did them. I loved all people so much. Now I am so close to death. Death is all around me. I have been here [on Death Row] for what seems another lifetime already. Several other people in this place have been called out.

She went on to give an account of her younger days in Germany and then described how her early setbacks in the US had led her into a life of crime.

My husband and I had been out of work and I started worrying about my boy's future. I became crazy with fears that my boy and I would starve. I signed some notes for my husband, because I had signed these notes they threatened to take my Colerain Avenue house away from me, to sell the house over my head and throw me and my boy out into the street. Then it was that I started gambling and playing the racehorses. I wanted to make some money for my boy.

Hahn met Palmer at the racetrack. She borrowed money from him.

I paid much of it back. Then when I didn't pay it back fast enough to suit him, then it was that he wanted me to be his girl. He threatened me that if I didn't do what he asked he would get his attorney to get the rest of the money that I borrowed from him. He wouldn't leave me alone. God knows that I did not want to kill him, and I don't know what put such a thought in my head. I remembered that down in the cellar was some rat poison. Something in my mind kept saying to me, 'Give him a little of this and he won't trouble you anymore'.

She put the poison in his oysters and told him to go home. Later she visited him in hospital and prayed he would get well. When he died, 'only I knew why'.

Still short of money, she had stolen some of Jacob Wagner's bank books. When he found out, she was frightened he would report her.

> I got scared that if the police would start questioning me maybe all this about Mr Palmer would come out. Something cried out in me to stop him, so that all my troubles wouldn't start again. I don't know what guided my hand, but I fixed him some orange juice and placed a half a teaspoon of the powder poison, which I took from my purse, in the glass.

She claimed that she did not kill Wagner for his money. Forging his will was an afterthought, she said. She also admitted killing George Gsellman and George Obendorfer, but did not give details.

> I have written this confession with the full knowledge that death is near, and I only ask one favour and that is that my son should not be judged for the wrongs his mother may have done.

The confession was signed Anna Marie Hahn.

Execution

Once all of the appeals were exhausted, Anna Marie Hahn was escorted from her cell with one of her counsels and her three matrons. As she was marched through the death house, the 12 convicted men awaiting their own executions paid their respects.

'Goodbye all of you and God bless you,' she said.

Approaching the door of the execution chamber, she stumbled and two guards had to pick her up and put her in the chair. Only then did she beg for mercy. Turning to the prison warden, she said: 'Mr Woodward, don't do this to me. Think of my boy. Can't you think of my baby?'

Then she addressed the witnesses to her execution, saying: 'Isn't there anybody who will help me? Is nobody going to help me?'

'I'm sorry, but we have to do it, Mrs Hahn,' replied the warden.

She beckoned to the chaplain, the Reverend John Sullivan, saying: 'Father, come close.'

He gripped her hand, but she whispered between sobs: 'Be careful, father. You will be killed.'

The Reverend Sullivan then intoned the Lord's Prayer as the current crackled through her body at 8.10 p.m. on 7 December 1938. Three minutes later she was declared dead.

JOSEF MENGELE

Dr Josef Mengele's insatiable appetite for cruelty exceeded that of the most cold-blooded mad doctors of pulp fiction. The murderous Nazi was known as the 'Angel of Death' because of the many sadistic experiments he carried out on the helpless inmates of Auschwitz concentration camp during World War II.

Mengele selected who was to work and who was to die – he was personally responsible for the murder of 400,000 people, many of them children.

Mengele's name and the enormity of his crimes was unknown to the Allies when they liberated the concentration camps in 1945, allowing the 'Angel' to slip unnoticed through the chaos of post-war Europe and seek asylum in South America. It was only in 1961, after the dramatic arrest and abduction from Argentina of Adolf Eichmann, the architect of the 'Final Solution', to stand trial for war crimes that the search for Mengele was intensified. But it would be another 24 years before one of the most notorious mass murderers in history was finally located.

Burial site

In 1985, impelled by a fresh American initiative to bring Mengele to justice, two German expatriates domiciled in Brazil offered to take investigators to what they claimed was the burial site of the world's most wanted war criminal.

Naturally, both the American and German authorities demanded that their forensic experts be allowed to examine the remains and determine the identity of the man who had been buried under the name of Wolfgang Gerhard. But there was an additional group with claims to a special interest in the outcome – associates of the celebrated Nazi-hunter Simon Wiesenthal, who had himself been an inmate of Auschwitz. Together the three parties assembled a distinguished team of experts who travelled to the remote Brazilian town of Embu on 6 June 1985.

There they exhumed the coffin and examined its contents, which were evidently those of a white, right-handed elderly male between 60 and 70 years of age. These basic facts could be determined by the narrowness of the pelvis, the shape of the skull, the comparatively longer bones on the right side and the degree of wear of the teeth and specific bones. A more accurate estimate of the age of the skeleton was

Josef Mengele (centre) with other SS officers on the grounds of Auschwitz.

indicated by the multitude of microscopic canals in the femurs which carry the blood vessels. The amount and condition of these indicated a man in his late sixties, which would correspond to Mengele's age. The length of key bones gave a reliable height for the corpse of 173.5 cm (5 ft 7 in), half a centimetre short of the height recorded in Mengele's SS file. But his dental record proved to be of little use as it was hand-drawn and light on detail, although it indicated a gap at the front of the upper palate which resulted in a characteristic gap-tooth grin. An X-ray of the skull confirmed that 'Herr Gerhard' had possessed the very same distinctive feature.

No doubt

In the final stage of the examination the skull provided the conclusive evidence. Using a technique known as video superimposition, the German forensic anthropologist Richard Helmer overlaid a photograph of the skull on to archive photographs of Dr Mengele to reveal 30 key features that were a positive match.

Nevertheless, there were those who feared the Angel of Death had eluded them yet again. Finally, in 1992 the advent of genetic fingerprinting made it possible to compare DNA from the remains in Embu with a sample from one of Mengele's living relatives. There could be no doubt – the bones in Brazil were those of Dr Mengele.

MARCEL PÉTIOT

Dr Marcel Pétiot's crimes, among the most grisly in European history, were motivated by nothing but greed. As he walked to the guillotine in Paris on 26 May 1946, he is said to have remarked, 'When one sets out on a voyage, one takes all one's luggage with one.'

This was not a privilege given to any of his more than 60 victims. For at his trial two months before, the jury had been shown 47 suit-cases that belonged to the men and women he had murdered – containing over 1,500 items of their clothing. All had been found at his death house on the rue Lesueur.

Pétiot, born in 1897 in Auxerre, was, it later transpired, a childhood sadist who stole from his schoolmates, and while serving at a casualty clearing-station in World War I, started out on another career: selling drugs. He qualified as a doctor in 1921, and soon set up shop in the village of Villeneuvesur-Yonne, where he made a reputation for himself as a drugs-supplier and provider of illegal abortions. As a result of dogged canvassing on his part, he was elected mayor in 1928, by which time he'd married. But question-marks began to gather about the doctor. He was caught stealing twice – and there was worse. Screams were heard coming from his surgery late at night. His housekeeper became pregnant and then disappeared. Later, a woman patient was robbed and killed; and another patient, who persisted in accusing the doctor of being responsible, suddenly died – of 'natural causes,' wrote the doctor on the death certificate.

All this persuaded Pétiot to up sticks to Paris, where he took up what came to be a successful practice in the rue Caumartin. Outwardly, again, he was respectability itself, with a wife and child; and no doubt it was this that enabled him to survive charges, once more, of shoplifting and drug-dealing, for which he received only fines. He was popular with his patients, and no one seemed to pay any attention when, after the German occupation of Paris, he bought another house on the rue Lesueur and started having it rebuilt to his own specifications.

The rebuilt house contained a new furnace in the basement beneath the garage, and an airtight triangular room with peepholes let into the door, 'for my mental patients,' said Dr Pétiot. It was, in fact, for something a lot more sinister. For once the house had been finished, he put out word that he was in touch with the French Resistance, and could smuggle people out of Paris.

He immediately had customers, among the first a rich Jewish businessman and his family, who paid him two million francs for his help. He treated them exactly the same as all the others who were to follow – Jews, Resistance fighters, those on the run from the Gestapo: he gave them an injection of poison – the injection was to protect them against typhus, he said – and watched them die behind the peepholes in the airtight room. He then treated their bodies in quicklime, bought in bulk from his brother in Auxerre, and burned what was left of them in the furnace below. In each case – and there were 63 of them – he kept scrupulous records of the furs, cash, jewellery and precious metals his 'clients' had brought with them to take into exile.

It was the furnace which in the end proved Pétiot's undoing. For in March 1944, a neighbour complained about the smoke that was billowing from it and called the police and the fire brigade. The police

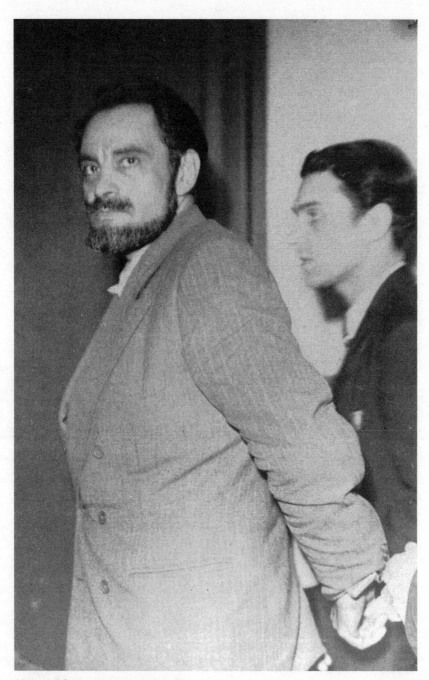

Marcel Pétiot at his trial in 1946.

went off to find the doctor at his house on the rue Caumartin. But the firemen broke in, and soon found the furnace surrounded by dismembered corpses. The doctor, though, when he arrived at the scene, had a plausible and patriotic explanation: they were the bodies, he confided, of Nazi soldiers and of collaborators condemned to death by the Resistance, for which he was working.

The French gendarmes, half convinced, returned to their headquarters without him; and he, his wife and 17-year-old son immediately fled before senior officers demanded – as they later did – a proper search of the premises. Once Paris was liberated a few weeks later, Pétiot became France's most wanted man. But instead of leaving the country, he belatedly joined the Free French forces and hand-wrote a letter to a newspaper saying as much, adding that he'd been framed by the Gestapo. A handwriting check soon established who he'd become, a Captain Valéry serving in Reuilly. He was arrested and after 17 months in captivity he came to trial, charged with murdering the 27 people whose remains the firemen had found.

One intriguing suggestion is that Pétiot at one time himself aroused the suspicions of the Gestapo – who arrested him as what he proclaimed himself to be: a member of the Resistance involved in smuggling people out of Paris. He was freed on the grounds that, in murdering Jews and people on the run, he'd simply been doing their work for them.

NANNIE DOSS

Many serial killers have been driven by perverted ideas of sex. Nannie Doss may be one to have been driven by a perverted notion of romance. When investigators asked this mild-looking grandmother about the four husbands she had murdered (among at least ten victims in all), she explained her actions by saying: 'I was looking for the perfect mate, the real romance of life.'

Another 'tragedy'

Nancy 'Nannie' Doss was born in the rural town of Blue Mountain in the hill country of north-west Alabama in 1905. She had a tough childhood. Her father James Hazle was an authoritarian farmer who worked his children as if they were hired farmhands and beat them if they failed to keep up with his demanding pace of work. Despite, if not because, of her father's strictness, Nannie became a wilful teenager, known for her promiscuity. In 1921, aged 16, she married a co-worker at the Linen Thread Company, Charles Braggs, and they had four children in quick succession. Nannie jumped into the relationship to escape her domineering father but found herself living with her new husband's equally domineering mother. When Charles himself turned out to be a drunk and a womanizer, Nannie responded by going back to her wild ways.

The marriage clearly was not built to last and it came to an end with what appeared to be a double tragedy. In 1927 the couple's two middle children both died in separate episodes of suspected food poisoning. At the time no one suspected foul play, but soon afterwards Charles Bragge ran off, taking their eldest daughter with him. He later claimed that he was frightened of his wife and had made a point of not eating anything she prepared.

With her husband gone, Nannie took a job at a cotton mill to support herself and her remaining daughter, Florine. In due course she moved across the state line to Georgia and remarried, to a man named Frank Harrelson. Harrelson turned out to be another alcoholic ne'er-do-well, although the relationship persisted until 1945 when another apparent tragedy struck. Once again a child died. This time it was Florine's daughter, Nannie's granddaughter. Florine had left her infant son with her mother while she visited her father. Three days later the baby was dead. The suggestion was that he might accidentally have swallowed rat poison.

Three months later, Nannie claimed her first adult victim. Frank Harrelson came home drunk and abused her one time too many. The next day, she put rat poison in his corn liquor. Several agonized days later he was dead, and, once more, no one suspected a thing.

Fortunately for Nannie, she had recently insured Frank's life and she now used the payment to buy a house in Jackson, Mississippi, where she lived until 1947. At this point, Nannie answered a lonely hearts advertisement – romance magazines and lonely hearts columns were Nannie's favoured reading matter – placed by a man named Arlie Lanning from Lexington, North Carolina. Two days after they met, they were married. However, once again Nannie's new husband proved to be a disappointment. Arlie was another drunk, and after three years Nannie had had enough of him.

In February 1950 Nannie served Arlie a meal of stewed prunes and coffee. He had terrible stomach pains for two days, and then died. Nannie told the neighbours that his last words were: 'Nannie, it must have been the coffee.' Of course, he may have been wrong: it may have been the arsenic in the coffee, but then again it could have been the prunes, that had been stewed in rat poison. The doctor, needless to say, did not suspect murder, not even when their house – which would have gone to Arlie's sister in his will – mysteriously burnt down, leaving Nannie with the insurance payment.

As soon as the insurance cheque cleared, Nannie left town. She visited her sister Dovie – who promptly keeled over. In 1952 Nannie signed up to a new innovation, a dating agency called the Diamond Circle Club. Through the agency Nannie met Richard Morton from Emporia, Kansas. Yet again he proved a disappointment, not a drunk this time, but a fraud and a womanizer. He was not to be her next victim, however: that was her mother Louise, who came to stay in January 1953, fell ill with chronic stomach pains and died. Three months later, Richard Morton went the same way. Yet again the doctors failed to ask for an autopsy.

Poisoned romance

During her brief marriage to Morton, Nannie had continued corresponding with her lonely hearts, and immediately after the funeral she went to Tulsa, Oklahoma, to meet the likeliest new prospect, Samuel Doss. They were married in June 1953. Doss was not a drinker or womanizer: he was a puritanical Christian and a miser. Once again, Nannie's new husband failed to meet her romantic ideal. A little over a year later, in September 1954, shortly after eating one of Nannie's prune cakes, Samuel was admitted to hospital with stomach pains. He survived and was released from hospital 23 days later. That evening, Nannie served him a perfectly innocent pork roast, which he washed down with a cup of coffee laced with arsenic. He died immediately, and this time the physician ordered an autopsy.

They found enough arsenic to kill 20 men in Samuel's stomach. The police confronted Nannie, unable to believe that this 50-year-old grandmother could be the killer. She unnerved them by giggling at

Nannie Doss's police mugshot, taken in Tulsa in October 1954.

their questions; then, when they refused to let her continue reading her romance magazine, she confessed to killing not just Samuel but her previous three husbands as well.

The news was an immediate sensation. The press dubbed Nannie the 'Giggling Granny' and she was put on trial for murder. She was duly sentenced to life in prison and, after serving ten years of her sentence, died in 1965, aged 60. Further investigation revealed that Nannie's four husbands, two children and granddaughter were not the only victims; Nannie's mother, two sisters, a nephew and a grandson had also died of arsenic poisoning.

JOHN BODKIN ADAMS

onvicted of fraud in the 1950s, Eastbourne general practioner John Bodkin Adams was acquitted of murder, though in ten years of practice 163 of his patients died while in a coma and 132 left him money or valuables in their wills. Most were elderly and seem to have been eased out of this life with pain killers. In those days, this may have been considered as kindness or perhaps euthanasia. Today it would be considered murder.

In 1957, Adams stood trial for the murder of wealthy widow, 81-year-old Edith Alice Morrell, who had been partially paralyzed after she had suffered a stroke in June 1948 and was only expected to live another six months. She survived over two years in Adams's care. Three months before she died on 13 November 1950, she added a codicil to her will saying that he was to receive nothing from her estate. Nevertheless, while maintaining that Mrs Morrell had died of natural causes – a second stroke – Adams inherited a chest of silver cutlery and a Rolls-Royce which was given to him by her son Claude. There was also payment of an outstanding bill for £1,674 for healthcare, which was later disputed.

As Mrs Morrell's death was not sudden, violent or unnatural, there was no inquest. Claude arranged for her to be cremated and her ashes scattered over the English Channel. Adams had to complete a medical certificate before the cremation. One question was: 'Have you, so far as you are aware, any pecuniary interest in the death of the deceased?' He wrote: 'No.' Otherwise there would have had to be a post-mortem.

Suspected barbiturate poisoning

Nearly six years later, suspicion was cast on Adams after 50-year-old Gertrude Hullett died under his care. She was depressed after the death of her husband, another of Adams's patients, and was prescribed barbiturates. An inquest found that she had committed suicide, though the coroner criticized Adams, saying that, knowing Hullett's history, it was extraordinary that he did not 'at once suspect barbiturate poisoning'.

Another suspicious circumstance around Hullett's death was that, on 17 July 1956, she had made out a cheque to him for £1,000. However, when the bank told him it would not clear until the 21st, he asked for special clearance so the funds would appear in his account the following day. Mrs Hullett died on 19 July. She also left him her Rolls-Royce in a will written five days before she died. He sold it six days before he was arrested.

The people of Eastbourne already had their suspicions. Born into Plymouth Brethren, an austere Protestant sect, Adams studied medicine in Belfast. In 1922, he moved to Eastbourne where he lived with his mother Ellen and his cousin Sarah Henry. Seven years later, he borrowed £2,000 (worth £130,000 in 2020) from a patient named William Mawhood and bought an upmarket mansion. Nevertheless he would invite himself to Mawhood's house for meals, bringing his mother and cousin. He also charged things to Mawhood's account without his permission. When Mawhood died in 1949, Adams allegedly stole a gold pen as a memento.

Adams's activities came to public attention on 1935, when he inherited over half of the estate of wealthy patient Matilda Whitton.

Her family contested the will, but it was upheld in court. Gossip spread that Adams was bumping off patients. At the time, Adams was giving his patient Mrs Agnes Pike morphine injections. When her health deteriorated, another doctor was called in and she made an almost full recovery.

During World War II, Adams worked in the local hospital as an anaesthetist, but was found to be incompetent. Nevertheless, in private practice, he manage to build up a wealthy clientele and was rumoured to be the richest GP in Britain.

After the death of Gertude Hullett, Scotland Yard was called in to investigate. Detective Superintendent Herbert Hannam had plenty to go on. Meeting Adams he remarked on the number of legacies the doctor had received. Adams said that a lot of what he received was in lieu of fees, claiming that money was of no interest to him.

'I paid £1,100 super tax last year,' he said.

Hannam mentioned that Gertrude Hullett's husband Alfred had left him £500, after Adams was thought to have despatched by him with morphine. Adams said he thought it would have be more. But Adams had again lied on the cremation forms that he had not inherited from the deceased. Adams's excuse was that he did not want to prevent the funeral going off smoothly for the relatives.

Speaking of the death of Mrs Morrell, Adams told Hannam: 'Easing the passing of a dying person isn't all that wicked. She wanted to die. That can't be murder. It is impossible to accuse a doctor.'

Adams's house was searched and dangerous drugs were found. He admitted that he did not keep a Dangerous Drugs Register as was required by law. He also admitted that he was in the practice of facilitating 'easing the passing' of terminally ill patients, something which was common practice at the time.

Hannam and his team investigated the cases of the 132 patients where Adams had benefitted from the decease's will and submitted a short list of 14 to the Department of Public Prosecutions, who considered five warranted prosecution. These includes Mrs Morrell, Mr and Mrs Hullett, Julia Bradnum and Clara Neil Miller, though there were others that were more than a little suspicious.

Eighty-five-year-old Julia Bradnum had died in 1952 after Adams had suggested she rewrite her will. He received £661. Often he had been seen holding her hand or down on one knee talking to her. The day before she died she was seen to be well and active. The next morning, she felt unwell. He gave her an injection and three minutes later she was dead, but when her body was exhumed five years later it was too badly decomposed to discover the cause of death.

Adams treated 72-year-old Julia Thomas for depression after the death of her cat. He gave her sedatives. After more pills, she fell into a coma. He told Mrs Thomas's cook: 'Mrs Thomas has promised me her typewriter, I'll take it now.' She died at 3 a.m. the next morning.

Eighty-six-year-old Hilda Nell Miller died in February 1953 in the guest house where she lived with her sister Clara. They were cut off from their relatives. When Hilda's long-standing friend Dolly Wallis asked Adams about her health, he answered her in medical terms she said she did not understand. While visiting Hilda, Adams was seen by her nurse, Phyllis Owen, picking up articles in the room, examining them and slipping them in his pocket. Adams arranged Hilda's funeral and burial himself.

Adams often held his consultations with Hilda's 87-year-old sister Clara Nell Miller behind locked doors. He was, supposedly, comforting her. She died in February 1954, the coldest month in many years. He read the Bible to her in a room where the windows were left open, her bed clothes were pulled off and her nightgown pulled up over her chest. Adams was sole executor and inherited a large sum of money. Some £200 went to Annie Sharpe, Miller's landlady, who was the only other person to attend her funeral. Morphine and barbiturates were found in her body, but again it was too badly decomposed to draw conclusions.

Hannam interviewed Sharpe in November 1956, suspecting that she was in collusion in a money-making scheme with Adams and, hence, a key witness. But Adams diagnosed Sharpe with cancer. She died soon after and was cremated.

James Downs died aged eighty-eight in May 1955. He had entered a nursing home with a broken ankle four months earlier. Adams had treated him with a sedative containing morphine, which made him forgetful. On 7 April Adams gave his nurse, Sister Miller, a tablet to make him more alert. Two hours later, a solicitor arrived to amend his will. Adams told him he was to inherit £1,000. Nurse Miller later told police she had heard Adams earlier that April telling Downs: 'Now look Jimmy, you promised me... you would look after me and I see you haven't even mentioned me in your will. I have never charged you a fee'. Downs died after being in a coma for 36 hours, 12 hours after Adams's last visit. Adams charged his estate £216 for his services and signed Downs's cremation form, again stating he had 'no pecuniary interest in the death of the deceased'.

Death penalty

Adams was arrested on 24 November 1956 on 13 charges including false representation on cremation certificates and granted bail. The Director of Public Prosecutions then decided to proceed with the case of Mrs Morrell and on 19 December 1956 Adams was arrested again and charged with her murder. Initially he would stand trial for this murder alone, but the Attorney-General mooted that, if the prosecution succeeded, he would then stand trial for the murder of Mrs Hullett. If convicted for both, Adams would have faced the death penalty.

Told of the charges, he said: 'Murder... murder... Can you prove it was murder? I didn't think you could prove it was murder. She was dying in any event.'

The trial took place in Lewes under Lord Patrick Devlin. He had his misgivings with the prosecution case. Firstly, they had to prove that a murder had been committed – a difficult thing to do without a body. Secondly they would have to prove that Dr Adams had injected her with some poison or in some other way caused her death. Then they would have to prove that Adams had intended to kill her. Nevertheless, the case had already attracted so much press coverage that it was being billed 'the murder trial of the century' and 'one of the greatest murder trials of all time'.

The prosecution quickly ran into difficulties. Two of its lead witnesses were nurses who had worked alongside Adams. However, their testimony diverged from the notebooks they had kept at the time which the defence had somehow managed to get their hands on. The expert medical witnesses that the prosecution called failed to give coherent testimony, while the expert witness called by the defence said that Adams's methods were unusual but not reckless. Adams himself did not testify in his own defence.

In his summing up, Lord Justice Devlin said that a doctor needed no special defence and 'is entitled to do all that is proper and necessary to relieve pain even if the measures he takes may incidentally shorten life'. In the case of Mrs Morrell, or the other cases that Adams had a hand in, there was no chance that the patient could be returned to good health. The jury found Adams not guilty after just 44-minutes' deliberation.

The case for the murder of Mrs Hullett was then dropped in a peculiar manner. Normally, a cursory trial would have been allowed to proceed, Adams would have pleaded not guilty, the prosecution would have brought no evidence and Adams would have been acquitted. Instead the Attorney-General dropped the indictment using a procedure called *nolle prosqui* – Latin for 'unwilling to pursue'. This was usually only used in cases where a guilty party had been granted immunity so they could turn Queen's evidence or that they were too gravely ill to stand trial.

After the trial Adams was paid £10,000 – the equivalent of £250,000 in today's money – for his life story, but he did not spend it. The notes were found in a bank vault untouched after his death. He resigned from the newly established National Health Service. In July 1957, he was convicted of eight counts of forging prescriptions, four counts of making false statements on cremation forms and three offences under the Dangerous Drugs Act, and fined £2,400 plus costs of £457. His licence to prescribe dangerous drugs was revoked and he was struck off the Medical Register. However, four years later he was reinstated and returned to practice. He died in 1983.

In 1985, Sir Patrick Devlin, the judge, stated that Adams may have been a 'mercenary mercy killer' but, though compassionate, he was at the same time greedy and 'prepared to sell death'. Adams never thought he was doing anything wrong. Those whose lives he took were by-and-large elderly and terminally ill. He thought he was doing the best for his patients, though admittedly reaping a handsome reward.

Superintendent Hannam complained of high-level interference with the prosecution. He, in turn, was investigated for his relationship with the press. His police career was soon at an end and he went to work for a private security agency.

LILA AND WILLIAM YOUNG

f the accusations against Canadian 'baby farmers' Lila Gladys and William Peach Young are true, the couple must surely qualify as two of the most heartless killers in history. And yet, against all the odds and in spite of all the evidence accumulated against them, they evaded arrest and prosecution for their crimes.

The daughter of devoutly religious parents, Lila had lived an uneventful life until she met and married William Young, an Oregon-born medical missionary in the Seventh-Day Adventist Church. William had failed to qualify as a doctor, but he seemed undeterred by the fact. On the contrary, he was convinced an unshakeable belief in his 'calling' was all he needed to be able to practise medicine on the unfortunate heathens. He could not have heard the call loud enough, though, because he did not venture further than Nova Scotia, where he and his new bride opened the Ideal Maternity Home and Sanitarium in February 1928 as 'an expectant mothers refuge'. Unwed mothers-to-be and those women seeking discreet births were promised 'no publicity' and somewhere to dispose of their unwanted progeny.

It was an offer that soon brought clients from all over the state. The couple's desperate clients thought the term 'disposal' was a euphemism for the arranging of a discreet adoption, but the Youngs were not humanitarians by nature and they had no intention of spending their fees on the long-term care of the infants in their charge.

Their services and their silence did not, of course, come cheap. Married women were required to pay $75 for two weeks' stay at the Sanitarium, while single mothers were charged as much as $200, plus $12 for sundry items such as nappies and $2 a week for nursing while the adoption was being arranged. But the most lucrative item was the $20 charge for infant funerals, of which there were many – far more in fact than could possibly be attributed to natural causes. The Youngs paid local handyman Glen Shatford 50 cents to despatch the babies. He placed the infant in a butterbox obtained from the grocery store before burying it in waste ground. Shatford later confessed to burying up to 125 infants in a field owned by Lila's unsuspecting parents. Other children were more fortunate. They were farmed out to neighbours, who kept them alive for as long as they could on the mere $3 a week provided by the callous couple. For this long-term bed and board the Youngs charged the mothers $300. Babies of mixed-race parentage and those with disabilities were allegedly starved to death on a diet of water and molasses, presumably in the belief that they were being spared a fate worse than death.

More cost-cutting measures were adopted by the Youngs. Poor girls were given the chance to work off their debt as domestic servants, which cut the costs of their upkeep and ensured that no outsiders could learn the truth of what was happening at the Sanitarium. Trained medical staff were excluded. Clients were billed for the services of two doctors, but in practice Lila acted as midwife while William knelt at the foot of the bed and prayed for the unfortunate sinner.

The Youngs' deviousness and deceit paid real dividends when it came to the fees they charged prospective parents, who willingly handed over up to $1,000 per child for a no-questions-asked adoption, a fee which had increased to $5,000 by the 1940s. By fleecing their clients at both ends of the baby chain the Youngs were estimated to have netted $3.5 million and by the outbreak of World War II they had moved into a 54-room mansion. This large building could house up to 70 infants in its nursery and there were private rooms for wealthier clients who were willing to pay a premium for privacy. And there were always additional 'windfalls' to be had from guilt-ridden young mothers who desperately wanted their babies back after they had changed their minds. The price of retrieval was said to be $10,000.

Things fall apart

By all accounts the bullish Lila saw her charges as a burden and she was brutal in her handling of the women who came under her care. In March 1936 the couple were charged with the manslaughter of a mother and her baby, but after a three-day trial both were acquitted for lack of evidence. It was not until nine years later that public health officials received so many complaints of insanitary conditions and neglect that they could no longer afford to ignore them. The Youngs' application for a licence to operate under the Maternity Boarding House Act of 1940 was turned down while the complaints against them were being investigated and in spring 1945 the United States Department of Immigration threatened to prosecute the couple for smuggling children across the Canadian border into the United States. Additional charges were brought for practising medicine without a licence, for which they were subsequently convicted, but Lila and William walked free after paying a token fine of $150. Another conviction for selling babies across the United States border followed in June, but again a modest fine of less than $500 was imposed and the Youngs returned to their lucrative baby farming business.

Greed and arrogance

Lila's greed and arrogance were ultimately her undoing. She countered the claims made by a local newspaper with a suit for harassment, but the press were not to be bullied or intimidated as easily as her staff.

The newspaper persuaded a number of witnesses to come forward with damning testimony at the hearing, which ensured that the claim for damages was summarily dismissed. Furthermore, the maternity home went out of business before the end of the year. After the Youngs had been exposed they were soon filing for bankruptcy to stave off the deluge of claims that followed. They were also forced to sell their property and move to Quebec.

In 1962 alcoholism and cancer claimed the life of William Young and Lila succumbed to leukaemia five years later. She was buried in a plot close to the unmarked graves of her tiny victims.

MARIE HILLEY

Blue Mountain, Alabama, does not exist any more. In 2003 the insignificant little mill town was absorbed into the neighbouring city of Anniston. Some say it barely existed in the first place. Its population had never risen above a thousand or two. However, in 1953 it suddenly found itself in the spotlight. It was the birthplace and hometown of Nannie Doss, one of the country's most notorious and active serial killers. Three decades later, the people of Blue Mountain would learn that their tiny community had spawned another female serial killer.

Audrey Marie Frazier was born on 4 June 1933, 18 years after Nannie Doss. Her parents, Huey and Lucille Frazier, worked in the local mills, like nearly everyone in Blue Mountain. In fact, Marie's mother was employed by the Linen Thread Company, where Nannie Doss had once worked. Because Marie was an only child, she was in a better situation than many of her playmates. Whereas most of them came from large families of limited means, Marie's parents were able to do a little bit more for her.

Very early in life, Marie had decided that she would rise above the bleak life that her parents lived. She was determined to complete high school, a rare accomplishment in Blue Mountain, and then become a secretary. In 1945, the year that she reached the age of 12, the family moved 3.2 km (2 miles) down the road to Anniston. The move was a significant one for Marie. She would now attend Quintard Junior High School.

Whereas her old classmates had been the children of mill workers, she now attended classes with the sons and daughters of the mill owners. She adapted well to her new surroundings – her grades were high and she joined the student council. At the end of her first year, she was named 'Prettiest Girl at Quintard' in the high school yearbook.

When she left Quintard to go on to Anniston High School, it seemed obvious that the academically-gifted Marie would complete her secondary school education. Still intending to become a secretary, she joined the Commercial Club, an organization for those planning careers in the field. As she progressed from grade to grade, always achieving good marks, it seemed that other possibilities were opening up – she became a member of the Future Teachers of America.

Turning heads

By the time she entered her final years at Anniston High School, the 'Prettiest Girl' had become a beautiful young woman. Marie attracted a great deal of polite male attention in the school hallways, though her eyes fell on just one boy. His name was Frank Hilley and he was the son of a factory worker. He did not come from one of the mill-owning families. Even so, Frank tried his best to treat Marie as well as his circumstances would allow. He gave her gifts – whatever he could afford – and treated her to evenings out on the town.

Frank was a year older than his girlfriend, so he graduated from high school first. He then joined the Navy and was sent off to Guam. In May 1951 Frank took advantage of his first leave and married Marie. Because she was in her final months of high school, she stayed behind while her new husband crossed the country to his new assignment in

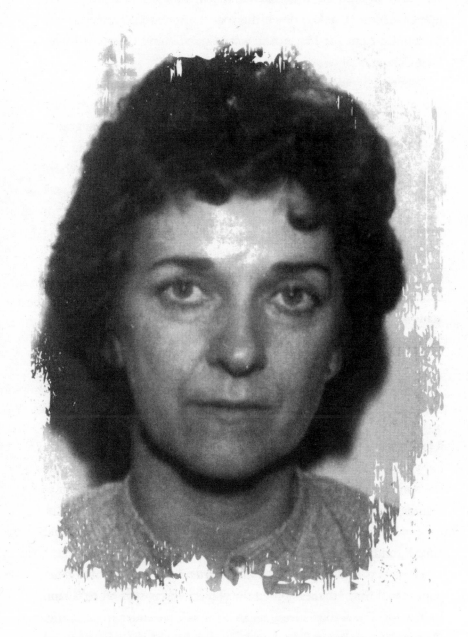

History repeats itself: Marie Hilley was the second female serial killer to emerge from the tiny town of Blue Mountain.

Long Beach, California. Frank sent his pay cheques home to Marie, but he was unaware that she was spending all of the money. As a result, the couple had no funds when the time came for her to join him on the West Coast. It fell to Marie's new in-laws to pay for her trip.

Marie's extravagance continued in California, which led to the first serious rows of their marriage. Then in 1952 the couple moved to Boston, where Frank completed his tour of duty and was discharged. Marie was in the early weeks of pregnancy when she and her husband returned to Anniston. Fortunately, the couple were able to make a down payment on a modest house. Frank found work with Standard Foundry, while Marie got a job as a secretary – just as she had always intended.

On 11 November 1952, the couple's first child, Michael, or Mike, was born. Their second baby, Carol, would not arrive until 1960. The Hilleys did reasonably well in the intervening years. Frank was now foreman of the shipping department, while Marie had become an executive secretary. Though Frank had achieved a degree of stability in his employment, the same could not be said for his wife. Marie moved from job to job and company to company. Although her employers appreciated her qualities, she did not get on well with her colleagues. Marie combined a snobbish attitude with a twisted approach to office politics, which made her unpopular with her colleagues.

Nevertheless, she never seemed to want for work. No sooner had she left one job than another fell into her lap. But a foreman and a secretary could never earn enough to satisfy Marie's craving for the finer things in life. The couple lived within their means, but only just. However, while the Hilley children never wanted for material possessions, their father was the only one who paid them any attention. The feminine and proper Marie turned her back on the tomboyish Carol. When Frank tried to make up for his wife's coldness by developing a loving relationship with his daughter, Marie became jealous.

By 1971, Marie and Frank had reached their platinum wedding

anniversary – but the marriage was in a very unhealthy state. The bride of 20 years had taken to taunting her husband by telling him that she was receiving love letters from a number of men in Anniston. Marie had also been slowly bringing the family to the point of bankruptcy. She had even rented a post office box so that she could receive bills without her husband's knowledge. And then she began falling behind with payments. Unknown to Frank, who had a reputation for always meeting his obligations on time, she had taken out several loans. It was only when his wife began to default that Frank became aware of the situation. This revelation, which came to light in the autumn of 1974, was soon matched by another one. Shortly afterwards, Frank arrived home early one day to find his wife in bed with her employer.

Mystery affliction

The reason Frank left Standard Foundry early that day was that he had been feeling ill. Throughout the remainder of 1974 and into the new year, the shipping foreman's condition continued to deteriorate. Though he was prescribed all sorts of medications, Frank continued to vomit frequently and he experienced long periods of nausea. In the early hours of 23 May, he was found wandering about outside the house. He was taken to the hospital, where he was diagnosed with infectious hepatitis. In spite of being given a range of prescription drugs, his condition only deteriorated. Marie stayed by her husband's bedside. She was joined by Mike, their son, who was now a pastor. He was concerned that his father's hallucinations might cause him to leap out of the window.

In the early hours of 25 May, Mike left to collect his grandmothers, who wanted to visit Frank. By the time he returned his father was dead. Marie had not witnessed Frank's final moments – she had apparently been asleep at the time. Because the cause of death was recorded as infectious hepatitis, Marie received $31,000 from her husband's insurance policies. It did not make her wealthy, but it funded a spending spree. She bought herself a car, a quantity of jewellery and some fine clothes. Others benefited too. Her mother was given a diamond ring and the children received cars, appliances and furniture.

Frank's death appeared to have set off a series of unfortunate, often mysterious events. Marie claimed that small items were being stolen from her home. After her mother was diagnosed with cancer, the old woman moved into the Hilley home. Marie convinced her son and daughter-in-law, Mike and Teri, to move in as well. But then Teri became very ill after experiencing severe bouts of stomach pain. She was hospitalized on four different occasions and she suffered a miscarriage.

Eventually, Mike and Teri decided to move out. However, a fire broke out at the Hilley house on the evening before they were due to take possession of their new apartment. While repairs were made, Mike and Teri were forced to share their apartment with Marie, Lucille and Carol. Weeks later, just as the three women were preparing to leave, a fire broke out in the neighbouring flat. So Mike and Teri were obliged to move back into the Hilley house with Marie, Lucille and Carol. Other fires followed. Shortly after her mother succumbed to cancer, Marie reported that someone had started a fire in one of her closets. Another closet fire was later reported by Marie's neighbour, Doris Ford. Marie told the police that she had been receiving calls of a threatening nature. Doris reported the same experience.

When Mike and Teri moved to Pompano Beach, Florida, Marie thought it best to leave Anniston. She moved into her son and daughter-in-law's new home, but the arrangement only lasted a few months. After running up $600 on Mike's credit card, Marie returned to Anniston. Strangely enough, the peculiar chain of events began again. There were severed telephone lines and still more fires. In the midst of all of this, Marie began a long-distance relationship with Calvin Robertson, an old high school classmate who was now living in San Francisco. When he was informed that she had cancer, he sent money for treatment, which Marie promptly spent on expensive clothes. Eventually, the relationship came to an end when Robertson realized that he did not want to leave his wife.

In April of 1979, Marie's daughter Carol and her mother-in-law Carol (Carrie) Hilley were both attacked by bouts of nausea and vomiting. In the months that passed, Marie demonstrated a level of affection and solicitude that had been lacking during her daughter's childhood. The secretary became a regular visitor to her daughter's apartment. She cooked for her and she administered the medicines that had been prescribed for her mystery illness. Carol's health continued on its downward spiral until August. At that point, Marie was advised to take the young woman to a psychiatrist. When she did so, she informed the doctor that her daughter had been suicidal. After hearing that, he thought it best that Carol should be placed in the Carraway Methodist Hospital in Birmingham, where she was admitted to the psychiatric ward.

It was while her daughter was under observation that Marie was arrested for the first time. The charge had nothing to do with murder, attempted murder or arson. Marie had been writing bad cheques. Without Frank's salary, and with the money from his life insurance long gone, Marie had resorted to fraud to buy the material possessions she so desired.

Although she was released on bail, it started to become clear that life as she had known it was coming to an end. Mike had discovered that Marie had administered injections of some unknown substance to both his father and his sister. As a result, the pastor asked that his mother be kept away from Carol. Confronted with this request, Marie removed her daughter from the Carraway Hospital and took her to the University of Alabama Hospital in Birmingham. On 20 September, Marie was again arrested for bouncing cheques. This time, though, there was no bail. She was still in prison when toxicology reports indicated that Carol had for some time been suffering from arsenic poisoning.

Six days after her arrest on the cheque charges, Marie admitted that she had given injections to her mother and her daughter. However, she claimed that the substance had been medicine supplied to her by the mother of a nurse. In October, Frank's body was exhumed. Tests revealed the presence of arsenic. The police then discovered a bottle of the poison at an address in Anniston. Marie had lived there for a while when she returned from Florida. Then a pill bottle containing arsenic was found in Marie's handbag after she was arrested. Finally, Lucille's body was exhumed. No one was surprised when the poison was once more identified.

As the authorities continued their investigation, they charged Marie with attempting to murder Carol. On 11 November 1979, after being released on bail, Marie was driven to a Birmingham motel by her attorney, Wilford Lane. After a few days, she asked to be moved to another location. She feared the vengeance of Frank's sisters. Meanwhile, the condition of Frank's mother continued to decline. On 18 November, her body weakened by arsenic poisoning, she died. That same day, Wilford Lane discovered that his client had disappeared. Her motel room, which showed the signs of a minor struggle, contained a rather melodramatic note. 'Lane, you led me straight to her. You will hear from me.'

Less than 24 hours later, Marie's aunt arrived home to find that her house had been burgled. Clothes and a suitcase had been stolen and her car was missing. A note had been left at this scene, as well. The burglars – for the note clearly read 'we' – told her not to worry; they would not be bothering her further. It was clear to everybody that both notes had been written by Marie. She had fled, but where to was the question.

A new identity

It is known that she somehow managed to make her way to Fort Lauderdale, Florida, where in February of 1980, she met a shy,

33-year-old divorcee named John Homan. At 46 years of age, Marie was considerably older than Homan but she solved the problem by adopting a new identity. The multiple murderer now presented herself as Robbi Hannon, a 35-year-old Texan. Within a year, the couple had married and moved to Marlow, New Hampshire, where Marie found employment at the Central Screw Corporation. Her story was intriguing. 'Robbi' was a Texan heiress whose two children had perished in a horrible automobile accident. Her story became sadder still when she revealed that she was dying of a rare blood disorder. Robbi's search for a cure led her to consult a number of out of town specialists. John stayed behind on these occasions. Then in September 1982, Robbi made a trip for an entirely different purpose. Her twin sister Teri was experiencing marital problems, so she had to fly to Texas to provide support. Robbi Hannon Homan was never seen again.

As it happened, Marie ended up in Florida. She bleached her hair, became 'Teri Martin' and began working as a secretary for a man named Jack McKenzie. It was not long before Marie was telling her new boss about Robbi, her ailing twin sister. On 10 November, Marie telephoned John Homan. Introducing herself as Teri Martin she informed him that Robbi had died. On the following day, the surviving twin appeared in Marlow. 'Teri' was thinner than 'Robbi' had been – and she was blonde. Because of that she fooled many people, including her husband John, who welcomed her into his home.

However, some of the workers at the Central Screw Corporation were not so sure. Several of them were certain that Robbi and Teri were one and the same person. When Teri placed an obituary for her deceased twin in the local paper they did some checking. They discovered that the hospital in which 'Robbi' had died did not exist, nor did the church at which her 'funeral' had taken place.

When they were presented with these findings, the local police investigated further. They came to the conclusion that Teri, or Robbi, might be a woman named Carol Manning, who was wanted for robbing a bank. However, on 12 January 1983, after being arrested at her place of work, 'Teri Martin' revealed that her true name was Audrey Marie Hilley. A week later, Marie was back in Anniston, where she was tried for Frank's murder, as well as the attempted murder of her daughter. When faced with the evidence, the defence really stood no chance. Marie was found guilty. She received a life sentence for Frank's murder, with an additional 20 years for poisoning Carol.

On 9 June 1983, she began serving her sentence as a medium security prisoner at Alabama's Tutwiler State Women's Prison. Incredibly, two years later Marie became classified as a minimum security prisoner, which made her eligible for day passes and periods of leave. By 19 February 1987, she had qualified for a three-day pass. That same weekend she met John Homan in an Anniston hotel room. Still smitten with the woman he had known as Robbi and Teri, he had been looking forward to spending a weekend with her. On Sunday morning, Marie left the hotel after telling John that she wished to visit her parents' graves. When she did not return, he went back to the hotel and found a note. 'I hope you will be able to forgive me,' it read. 'I'm getting ready to leave. It will be best for everybody. We'll be together again. Please give me an hour to get out of town.' Marie went on to say that she was flying to Canada and would contact him later.

But the fugitive never got there. On 26 February, four days after she had disappeared, Marie turned up in Blue Mountain, just a few minutes away. She was suffering from hypothermia and it was too late to revive her. Why was she there? Had somebody arranged to help her escape? Nobody knows.

GENENE JONES

There are 'Angels of Death' – nurses who work with old people and kill them as they approach the end of their lives. Then there are 'Death Nurses' who kill babies and young children who have hardly started theirs. Genene Jones fell into the second category, killing maybe as many as 50 infants.

Born in Texas in 1950, she was immediately given up for adoption. Her new parents, Gladys and Dick Jones, had three other adopted children, two older than Genene, one younger. They lived in a comfortable four-bedroom house in the suburbs of San Antonio. Her adoptive father Dick ran a nightclub until, when Genene was ten, he was arrested. A safe had been stolen from the house of a man who was in Jones's nightclub at the time of the burglary. When the safe turned up, Jones was suspected. He confessed, but claimed that the theft was a practical joke and charges were dropped. The nightclub then foundered. He opened a restaurant which also failed. Then he took to erecting billboards.

Through the resulting family tribulations, Genene felt overlooked and began calling herself the 'black sheep' of the family. To get attention, she feigned illness. At school she was shunned for being aggressive and manipulative. She was also short and overweight, which did not help.

Her closest companion was her younger brother Travis, two years her junior. When he was 14, he was making a pipe bomb that blew up in his face and killed him. A traumatized Genene screamed and fainted at the funeral.

A year later, her adoptive father died of cancer and her mother took to drink. To escape the family tragedies, Genene sought to marry. Underage, her mother would not allow it. Eventually, when she graduated, she married a high-school dropout who, after seven months, enlisted in the US Navy. She then began a series of affairs with married men. The couple divorced after four years while her husband was in hospital after an accident. The divorce papers indicate that it had been a violent relationship.

No love like a mother's love

Claiming that she had always wanted children, Genene Jones had two, but left them to be brought up by her mother, while she enrolled at beauty school. Fearing that hair dyes might give her cancer, Jones changed course. Having a penchant for medicine and doctors, she trained to become a Licensed Vocational Nurse, or LVN.

Her first job at San Antonio's Methodist Hospital lasted just six months. She was fired for making decisions that she was not qualified to take. Another job lasted little longer. Then she was hired by Bexar County Medical Center Hospital to work in their paediatric unit.

The first child she took care of had a fatal intestinal condition. When he died shortly after surgery, Jones broke down. She brought a stool into the cubicle where the body lay and sat staring at it. The other nurses could barely understand this. She hadn't known the child long and her grief seemed excessive.

Needing to be needed, she took care of the sickest children on the long 3–11 p.m. shift. It soon became known as the 'Death Shift'. Jones skipped classes on the proper handling of drugs and, in her first year, made eight elementary nursing errors, some concerning the dispensing of medication. Never liking to admit mistakes, she was bossy, telling other nurses what to do.

Foul-mouthed and always bragging about her sexual conquests, Jones was disliked by colleagues who regularly applied for transfers to get away from her. However, the head nurse Pat Belko protected her, even when she turned up for work drunk. She also upset new nurses by predicting which babies were going to die.

'Tonight's the night,' she would say. In one week, seven children died, often from conditions that should not have been fatal. Jones took a special interest in children that were near death and liked to be there when it happened, taking special pleasure informing and commiserating with the parents.

There were also numerous cases of children slipping into critical conditions in her care, then reviving during dramatic medical interventions. One child had a seizure three days in a row, but only on Jones's shift.

'They're going to start thinking I'm the Death Nurse,' Jones quipped.

Others thought so too, but Pat Belko sought to quash rumours that she was doing something to the children. This was just spiteful tittle-tattle from jealous colleagues, she maintained.

When Dr James Robotham became medical director of the paediatric unit, he took a more hands-on approach, leaving less for junior nurses to do. However, Jones ingratiated herself and basked in the attention he gave her.

She also sought attention by her old ruse of feigning illness, referring herself to the outpatients' unit 30 times in two years. This behaviour is now recognized as Munchausen's Syndrome.

Then, a six-month-old baby named Jose Antonio Flores went into cardiac arrest while in Jones's care. He was revived, but went into arrest again the next day during her shift and died from internal bleeding. Tests on the corpse indicated an overdose of a drug called heparin, an anticoagulant. No one had prescribed it.

At the news of his son's death, the child's father had a heart attack. After helping the father to the emergency room, Jones seized the dead baby and made off down the corridor with the family in pursuit. She gave them the slip and delivered the dead child to the morgue. Nobody could explain this bizarre behaviour.

Being treated for pneumonia, Rolando Santos began having seizures, cardiac arrest, and extensive unexplained bleeding. This started, then intensified on Jones's shift. In a coma, blood came up into his throat and his blood pressure dropped dangerously. But after he was removed from the paediatric ICU and put under 24-hour surveillance, he survived.

Another child was sent to the paediatric unit to recover from open-heart surgery. Although he progressed well at first, on Jones's shift his condition deteriorated and he soon died. Jones grabbed a syringe and squirted fluid over the child in the sign of a cross, then did the same again on herself. Grabbing the dead baby, Jones began to cry.

Two resident physicians treating a three-month-old boy named Albert Garza suspected that Genene had probably given him an overdose of heparin. When they confronted her, she got angry, but after their intervention the child recovered. Following this incident tighter control was applied to the use of heparin, making nurses more accountable.

While Genene's health was deteriorating, at least according to her own account, she refused to take the drugs she had been prescribed. Again, she seemed to be angling for attention. Her former ally Dr Robotham began to express concerns about Jones. However, in November 1981, the hospital administration had a meeting and decided that Robotham was over-reacting. They were not willing to invite the attention a formal investigation would garner. Nevertheless, Dr Robotham continued to keep an eye on the records of drug use on the 3–11 p.m. shift.

While the use of heparin was being monitored, 11-month-old Joshua Sawyer, who suffered a cardiac arrest after inhaling smoke during a fire at his home, was prescribed Dilantin, an anticonvulsant. While the doctors expected him to recover, Jones told his parents that it would be better to let him die as he would be suffering from brain damage. Suddenly, he had two more heart attacks and died. Tests showing a lethal dose of Dilantin in his blood were overlooked.

Finally, a committee was formed to look into the high mortality rate headed by Dr Robotham and Pat Belko. They decided not to put the blame on one nurse but to replace the LVNs on the unit with registered nurses, or RNs. That meant Jones would be transferred away from the paediatric unit. She promptly resigned.

A new life in a new town, but the deaths continue

In 1982, Dr Kathleen Holland opened a paediatric clinic in Kerrville, Texas. She hired Genene Jones, believing that she had been the victim of the male medical establishment at Bexar. Dr Holland had testified on Jones's behalf in the investigation and helped her move to Kerrville. However, she found she had bought into trouble. Children at the clinic began having seizures. In two months seven had to be transferred by ambulance to Kerr County's Sid Peterson Hospital, where the staff grew suspicious. In one case Jones was seen to inject something into the child. However, all recovered.

The first suspicious seizure happened on 17 September 1982, the very day the clinic first opened. The child was Chelsea McClellan, who had been born prematurely and was suffering from breathing problems. She was the clinic's first-ever patient. She had stopped breathing while in Jones's care, but she had placed an oxygen mask over the baby's face and they rushed her to an emergency room at the nearby Sid Peterson Hospital. To everyone's relief, the child recovered and Jones was showered with praise.

Nine months later, Chelsea returned to the clinic for a routine check-up and to have two inoculations. When Jones gave her the first, the child began having breathing difficulties. She had a seizure and her mother asked Jones to stop, but she went ahead and gave Chelsea the second injection anyway. She stopped breathing and was rushed to the Sid Peterson Hospital, but died in the ambulance on the way.

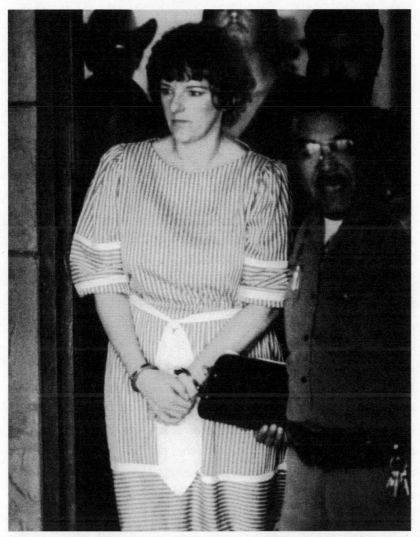

Genene Jones at a pre-trial hearing in 1984 – she was convicted of killing one infant, Chelsea McClellan, and nearly killing another, Rolando Santos, earning her a total of 159 years in prison.

Jones allegedly said: 'And they said there wouldn't be any excitement when we came to Kerrville.'

She sobbed over the child's body and lovingly wrapped it in a blanket before presenting it to the parents. The cause of death was given as SIDS – sudden infant death syndrome, or cot death.

A week after the funeral, Chelsea's grief-wracked mother Petti visited her daughter's burial site to find Jones kneeling at the foot of the grave, sobbing and wailing the child's name over and over as if Chelsea had been her own.

'What are you doing here?' asked Petti.

Jones stared at her blankly, as if in a trance, and walked away without a word. When she was gone, Petti McClellan noticed that Jones had left a small token of flowers, but had also taken a bow from Chelsea's grave.

Meanwhile, a committee had been formed at the Sid Peterson Hospital to investigate the deaths. They asked Dr Holland if she used succinylcholine, a powerful muscle relaxant. She said she kept some in her office but did not use it. The committee notified the Texas Rangers.

Jones then claimed that she had taken an overdose of doxepin, a drug used to fight anxiety, and had her stomach pumped. In fact, she had taken just four tablets, faking a coma, and was in no danger. Then a bottle of succinylcholine went missing and Dr Holland fired Jones.

Captured, but no rest for her victims' families – yet

On 12 October 1982, a grand jury in Kerr County investigated the death of Chelsea McClellan and the eight other children from Dr Holland's clinic who had developed emergency respiratory problems. Chelsea's body was exhumed and succinylcholine was found in the tissue. Her death had been caused by an injection of the muscle relaxant.

In February 1983, another grand jury was convened in San Antonio to look into the 47 suspicious deaths of children at the Bexar County Medical Center Hospital that had occurred while Genene Jones had been there. Chelsea's parents began a lawsuit against Jones and Holland, alleging wrongful death. Meanwhile, Jones married a 19-year-old boy, seemingly to deflect rumours that she was a lesbian.

The Kerr County grand jury indicted Jones on one count of murder and several charges of injury to seven other children who had been injected with muscle relaxants. Then the San Antonio grand jury indicted her for injuring Rolando Santos by deliberately injecting heparin. She remained a suspect in ten infant deaths at the hospital.

There were two separate trials. The prosecution alleged that the motive was Munchausen's Syndrome by Proxy – a psychological disorder where a caregiver indulges in attention-seeking behaviour by manipulating the health of their patients. Jones liked the excitement and the attention the sick children brought her. The children were at her mercy. They couldn't tell on her, so she was free to create the situation over and over again. There was no doubt that, over time, her actions had escalated and that she had taken more risks.

The first jury took just three hours to find Jones guilty of murdering Chelsea McClellan. She was given the maximum sentence of 99 years. Later, she was given another 60 years for injuring Rolando Santos. She had the possibility of parole, but the McClellans fought to keep her inside.

However, she was due for mandatory release in 2018 to avoid prison overcrowding. To prevent this, fresh charges were brought for the murder of Joshua Sawyer. The Bexar County District Attorney said that more murder charges would be levelled against her to prevent her release. In January 2020 Jones made a plea bargain with prosecutors by accepting guilt for the death of Joshua Sawyer in return for all other ongoing investigations against her being dropped.

DONALD HARVEY

Claiming some 87 victims, Donald Harvey is possibly America's most prolific serial killer. Working as a hospital orderly, he murdered patients in what he claimed were mercy killings. However, he also let his murderous ways spill out into his personal life.

On the surface there was little clue in his early life that Harvey would turn out a serial killer. His mother said that he had 'always been a good boy' and the principal of his elementary school said: 'He was always clean and well dressed with his hair trimmed. He was a happy child, very sociable and well-liked by the other children. He was a handsome boy with big brown eyes and dark curly hair... he always had a smile for me. There was never any indication of any abnormality.'

However, it appears that his parents had an abusive relationship. His father dropped him when he was just six months old, before the soft spot had closed. He suffered another head injury at the age of five when he fell off the running board of a truck. Although he did not lose consciousness, there was a cut 10–13 cm (4–5 in) long on the back of his head.

From the age of four he was sexually abused by his Uncle Wayne. A neighbour also sexually abused him, but Harvey did not mind this as the old man gave him money.

At high school, his classmates saw him as a teachers' pet who would rather have his nose stuck in a book than play sports. He did well academically, initially. But learning came too easily. He grew bored and dropped out. He had his first consensual sexual encounter when he was 16. The following year he began an on-off sexual relationship with James Peluso that lasted for 15 years.

With little direction in life, Harvey left Booneville, Kentucky, and moved to Cincinnati, where he got a job in a factory. In 1970, he was laid off. His mother asked him to visit his ailing grandfather who was in Marymount Hospital in London, Kentucky. Spending time there, he got to know the staff.

One of them asked Harvey if he wanted a job as an orderly. Unemployed at the time, he jumped at the chance. Though he had no medical training, his duties included passing out medication, inserting catheters and changing bedpans. The job meant he spent time alone with patients. Around that period, he claimed he was raped by his roommate.

An angry young man

While Harvey made out that he was a mercy killer, his first murder was motivated by anger. He later told Dan Horn of the *Cincinnati Post* that when he went to check on 88-year-old stroke victim Logan Evans in his private room, the patient rubbed faeces in his face. Harvey lost control.

'The next thing I knew, I'd smothered him,' he said. 'It was like it was the last straw. I just lost it. I went in to help the man and he wants to rub that in my face.'

Harvey put a sheet of blue plastic and a pillow over the old man's face and listened to his heartbeat with a stethoscope until he was dead. He disposed of the plastic and cleaned him up, dressing Evans in a fresh hospital gown. Then he had a shower before notifying the nurse on duty of Evans's death. Harvey had no fear of getting caught.

'No one ever questioned it,' he said.

The following day he said he accidentally killed 69-year-old James Tyree when he used the wrong-sized catheter on him. When Tyree yelled at him to take it out, Harvey silenced him with the heel of his hand. Tyree then vomited blood and died.

Three weeks later came the first of what could be considered mercy killings. Forty-two-year-old Elizabeth Wyatt told him she wanted to die, so he turned down her oxygen supply. Four hours later, a nurse found her dead.

The following month, he killed 43-year-old Eugene McQueen by turning him on his stomach when he knew he wasn't supposed to. McQueen drowned in his own fluids. Harvey told the nurse merely that McQueen looked bad and she told him to continue with his duties. Consequently, Harvey gave McQueen a bath even though he was already dead. For as long as he worked at Marymount, the staff teased Harvey for bathing a dead man.

He accidentally killed 82-year-old Harvey Williams when a gas tank proved faulty. But the next death at his hands was premeditated murder. Eighty-one-year-old Ben Gilbert knocked him out with a bedpan and poured its contents over him, saying that he thought Harvey was a burglar. Harvey retaliated by catheterizing Gilbert with a female-sized 20-gauge catheter instead of the smaller 18-gauge used for men. He then straightened out a coat hanger and shoved the wire through the catheter, puncturing Gilbert's bladder and bowel. Gilbert went into shock and fell into a coma. Harvey disposed of the wire and replaced the 20-gauge catheter with an 18-gauge. Ben Gilbert died four days later.

Harvey began a seven-month relationship with Vernon Midden, a married man who had children. He was an undertaker who taught Harvey the tricks of the trade and introduced him to the occult. When the relationship went sour the following January, Harvey fantasized about embalming him alive.

Killing as an act of kindness?

Maude Nichols had been so neglected that her bedsores crawled with maggots. When she arrived at Marymount, Harvey fixed her up with a faulty oxygen tank. He simply neglected to turn on the oxygen for 58-year-old William Bowling, who had difficulty breathing and subsequently died of a heart attack.

A faulty oxygen tank also did for 63-year-old Viola Reed Wyan after his attempt to smother her was interrupted. She had leukaemia and Harvey complained that she smelt bad. Ninety-one-year-old Margaret Harrison was despatched with an overdose of Demerol, morphine and codeine that was intended for another patient.

Harvey decided that 80-year-old Sam Carroll had suffered enough and he was given a faulty oxygen tank. Maggie Rawlins was smothered with a plastic bag. Both 62-year-old Silas Butner and 68-year-old John V. Combs were killed with faulty oxygen tanks after attempts to smother them had failed. Ninety-year-old Milton Bryant Sasser was killed with an overdose of morphine which Harvey had stolen from the nurse's station. Harvey tried to dispose of the syringe by flushing it down the lavatory, where it was found by a maintenance man. Harvey left Marymount Hospital soon after. He was still only 18.

Harvey then had his first heterosexual encounter. He got drunk with the daughter of the family he was staying with and they ended up naked. Nine months later she had a child, naming Harvey as the father, though he rejected any responsibility.

Depressed, Harvey tried to kill himself by setting fire to the bathroom of an empty apartment. He was arrested and fined $50. Then he was arrested on suspicion of burglary, though the police really wanted to question him about his involvement with the occult. During the interview, he admitted killing 15 people at Marymount Hospital, but they did not believe him.

He briefly enlisted in the US Air Force, but was discharged after trying to commit suicide. A further suicide attempt landed him in a

Veterans' Administration Hospital after his parents would not take him in.

In 1972, he started work at the Cardinal Hill Convalescent Hospital in Lexington, Kentucky. It is not thought he killed anyone there. For ten months he lived with Russell Addison. This was followed by a five-year relationship with Ken Estes.

In September 1975, he became a nursing assistant at the VA Hospital in Lexington. He tampered with the oxygen supply for Joseph Harris, possibly resulting in his death. Harvey also claimed he had a hand in the deaths of James Twitty, James Ritter, Harry Rhodes and Sterling Moore.

To be initiated into the local occult group, Harvey had to hook up with a woman, so they could then swap partners with another couple. This resulted in the conception of another child, though Harvey denied any responsibility once again. He also acquired a spirit guide named Duncan, a doctor during his lifetime, who now directed him to kill from beyond the grave.

Donald Harvey suffered a couple of serious head injuries when he was young. He was also sexually abused by his Uncle Wayne.

Poisonous relationship

In 1980, Harvey began dating Doug Hill. When they fell out, Harvey attempted to poison him by putting arsenic in his ice cream. In August, he moved in with Carl Hoeweler. When he found Carl was fooling around with other men, he put small doses of arsenic in his food to prevent him going out. Fearing that Carl's 'fag hag' friend Diane Alexander was trying to split them up, he gave her hepatitis-B serum stolen from the hospital. He also tried unsuccessfully to infect her with AIDS.

His 63-year-old neighbour Helen Metzger was also considered a threat and murdered with arsenic in her food, though Harvey contended he did not mean to give her a lethal dose. Her family got sick from leftovers served at the funeral. Carl's 82-year-old father Henry was also despatched by arsenic. Carl's brother-in-law Howard Vetter was killed accidentally, Harvey claimed, when he left wood alcohol in a vodka bottle. Harvey also murdered another neighbour, Edward Wilson, who he thought was a threat to his relationship with Carl Hoeweler. Wilson was despatched with arsenic in his Pepto-Bismol bottle.

Harvey killed Hiram Profitt accidentally, giving him the wrong dose of heparin. Former boyfriend James Peluso, then 65, asked Harvey to help him out if ever he could not take care of himself. Harvey put arsenic in his daiquiri.

After he joined the neo-Nazi National Socialist Party, Harvey was fired from the VA Hospital in 1985 for carrying a gun in his gym bag. Body parts which he intended to use in occult practices were also found. The following year, he started a new job at Daniel Drake Memorial Hospital in Cincinnati.

After six weeks, he smothered 65-year-old Nathan J. Watson with a bin bag after several thwarted attempts. Watson was semi-comatose and was fed through a gastric tube and Harvey said he didn't think anyone should live that way. He also believed Watson to have been a rapist.

Four days later, 64-year-old Leon Nelson was despatched the same way. A week after that 81-year-old Virgil Weddle was killed with rat poison. Cookies stolen from him were used in rites for Duncan. Rat poison was also used to kill Lawrence Berndsen the next day.

Harvey put cyanide in 65-year-old Doris Nally's apple juice. Sixty-three-year-old Edward Schreibesis got arsenic in his soup, though arsenic failed to kill Willie Johnson. Eighty-year-old Robert Crockett succumbed to cyanide in his IV. Sixty-one-year-old Donald Barney had cyanide injected in his buttocks, while 65-year-old James T. Wood was given cyanide in his gastric tube. Eighty-five-year-old Ernst C. Frey got arsenic the same way.

Eighty-five-year-old Milton Canter got cyanide in a nasal tube. Seventy-four-year-old Roger Evans ingested it in his gastric tube. Sixty-four-year-old Clayborn Kendrick got it the same way. More cyanide was injected into his testes.

Cyanide was given to 86-year-old Albert Buehlmann in a cup of water and to 85-year-old William Collins in orange juice. Seventy-eight-year-old Henry Cody had it fed through his gastric tube.

Following his break-up with Carl, Harvey was treated for depression and tried to kill himself by driving off a mountain road, injuring his head. Sixty-five-year-old Mose Thompson and 72-year-old Odas Day were despatched with solutions of cyanide, while 67-year-old Cleo Fish got it in her cranberry juice. Two other patients were given arsenic but survived, while 47-year-old Leo Parker succumbed to cyanide in his feed bag.

Eighty-year-old Margaret Kuckro got it in her orange juice, as did 76-year-old Stella Lemon. Sixty-eight-year-old Joseph M. Pike and 82-year-old Hilda Leitz were despatched with the adhesive remover Detachol. Forty-four-year-old John W. Powell was killed with cyanide in his gastric feeding tube. An autopsy was performed and the pathologist smelt bitter almonds – the characteristic aroma of cyanide. Three laboratories confirmed its presence and the Cincinnati Police Department was notified.

Harvey came under suspicion because of his sacking from the VA Hospital. He called in sick the day that staff were given polygraph tests. When questioned, he admitted killing Powell, saying he felt sorry for him and denied killing anyone else.

Pat Minarcin, then an anchor at WCPO-TV in Cincinnati, figured that if he had killed once he might have done it on other occasions. Digging into Harvey's past, he managed to link him to 24 murders, filling a half-hour special report.

Court-appointed defence attorney Bill Whalen cut a plea bargain. If the death penalty was taken off the table, he said, Harvey would confess to all the murders. In August 1987 in Ohio, Donald Harvey pleaded guilty to 24 counts of murder and was sentenced to three concurrent terms of life. That November in Kentucky he pleaded guilty to another nine murders, giving him another life sentence plus 20 years. In the end, the self-styled Angel of Death pleaded guilty to 37 murders, though he admitted many more.

Incarcerated in Toledo Correctional Institution, he was found badly battered in his cell on 28 March 2017 and died two days later. Fellow inmate James Elliott was charged with his murder.

GWENDOLYN GRAHAM AND CATHERINE WOOD

I t is a sad and sobering fact that not all nurses and doctors are caring and compassionate professionals who put the wellbeing of their patients first. Michigan nurses Gwendolyn Gail Graham, 23, and Catherine May Wood, 24, might have been qualified to care for the elderly but they were certainly not compassionate or caring by nature. Quite the opposite, in fact.

The two women first met at the Alpine Manor Nursing Home in Walker, Michigan in 1987 where Wood was employed as a head nurse and Graham as her assistant. They became lesbian lovers and practised asphyxia to heighten their sexual pleasure. One thing led to another and before long they were discussing strangling their patients for kicks, going so far as to choose victims whose initials would spell out M-U-R-D-E-R, just in case the police were too slow to catch on. But the elderly women Graham chose for her first victims put up such a struggle that she had to give up. Incredibly none of her intended victims alerted the other staff or accused Graham of assault.

Graham then chose a victim who would not fight back. She was a patient with Alzheimer's disease who was smothered to death with little effort, while Wood kept a lookout. The next victims were easy to despatch too. Wood stood guard outside their rooms, while Graham suffocated them with a washcloth. Money was not the prime motive, even though the helpless women were robbed of their jewellery – the pair were sexually aroused by killing. They frequently slipped into an empty bedroom to satiate their lust as they relived the grisly details.

While they were there they fingered the souvenirs they had stolen from the crime scene. They did not just take jewellery and other valuables. Often it was mundane items, such as the victim's dentures. More appalling was the revelation that they even experienced sexual stimulation while preparing the bodies in the mortuary.

Yet no one employed at the nursing home suspected that the pair were acting oddly. Even when they boasted of what they were doing, their confessions were dismissed as a sick joke.

All the while Wood had been the passive partner, acting as lookout while Graham did the grisly deed, but then Graham demanded that Wood take a turn. She refused, transferring to another shift to avoid being taunted by her former lover. Graham, however, was insatiable. She found another lesbian partner and then took a job in a hospital maternity unit in Texas. Wood broke down and confessed all to her ex-husband when she heard that Graham had threatened to kill one of the babies, but he would not believe her.

He refused to go to the police. It was not until a year later that he finally relented, at which point the terrible truth came to light.

Graham and Wood played their so-called 'murder game' for about three months, during which time it is thought that they murdered as many as 40 elderly patients, though they were initially charged with killing five. Wood bargained for a lenient sentence by turning state's evidence, laying all the blame on her dominant, sadistic former partner. Graham's defence counsel countered that Wood had invented the whole story in order to avenge herself on Graham for taking a new lover, but the jury was not buying it. Graham was convicted of first degree murder in all five cases and one count of conspiracy to commit murder, for which she received six concurrent life sentences, with no possibility of parole.

RICHARD ANGELO

American serial killer Richard Angelo always wanted to be a hero. An Eagle Scout, he signed up to become a volunteer fireman as soon as he was old enough. Neighbours remarked on his courage and few thought he would be responsible for a string of vicious murders in later life.

Angelo was born in Lindenhurst, Long Island, in 1962, the only child of Joseph and Alice Angelo. His father was a high school guidance counsellor and his mother a home-economics teacher in local schools. Angelo himself graduated from St John the Baptist Catholic High School in 1980. It was next door to the Good Samaritan Hospital where he went about his grisly business later. He attended the New York state university at Stoney Brook from September 1980 to June 1982 where he took various science courses. He then transferred to a two-year nursing programme at the State University at Farmingdale where he made the dean's honours list in all four semesters.

'He was a B student who graduated in good standing,' said the chair of the university's nursing department. Otherwise he kept a low profile and did not stand out.

'We didn't have any run-ins with him here,' said Sergeant Robert

Queen of the university campus police. 'When we heard his name we were shocked.'

After graduating, Angelo became as a registered nurse in May 1985. He worked briefly at two Long Island hospitals before moving to Florida with his parents who had retired. Unhappy there, he returned to Long Island where he rented a one-room apartment in a two-storey house in Lindenhurst and landed a job at Good Samaritan Hospital, in West Islip in Suffolk County, Long Island, in April 1987.

Graveyard shift

He worked mainly with cardiac patients in a small, 24-bed, intensive care ward. Being the new boy, he was given the graveyard shift from 11 p.m. to 7 a.m., though he never complained about the hours. In fact, they suited him as he could go about his work without scrutiny.

Given the nature of the patients on the ward, it was not surprising that some of them died. However, there were some unusual deaths in the autumn of 1987. Patients who appeared to be recovering well from surgical procedures were suddenly dying without apparent cause. Between 16 September and 11 October there were six suspicious deaths that left doctors puzzled. But then the killer made a mistake.

On 11 October, two postoperative patients died in a single day. Then a patient named Girolamo Cucich buzzed for a nurse. He reported that a bearded man had approached his bed, saying: 'I am going to make you feel better.' He then injected something into Cucich's IV. Cucich immediately felt a numbness spreading through his body and his breathing became laboured. Nevertheless, he had the strength to buzz for a nurse whose quick-thinking saved his life. She took a urine sample for analysis.

The police were called. The following day they questioned Angelo who was the only male nurse on the ward that night and he had a beard. Naturally he was a suspect.

On 14 October, the New York state Health Department issued a statement saying it 'did not identify any direct evidence linking the nurse under suspicion with the deaths... Incomplete record-keeping made it impossible to identify the personnel involved in each case.'

The statement went on: 'The Department did identify a number of cases in which a patient seemed to be progressing satisfactorily and then died for no clear, apparent reason. Whether or not these cases may have involved the nurse in question, the Department of Health believes these cases should have been identified by the hospital and investigated for potential quality of care problems. They were not.'

A spokesman for the Department said: 'We couldn't tell for sure about the cases and their own internal system was so bad they couldn't know what was happening. The quality assurance system of the hospital was inadequate and ineffective. Key components of a quality assurance system, such as the review of mortalities, morbidity and errors in diagnosis and treatment were not being conducted in any consistent manner.'

Lethal injection

By 3 November 1987 laboratory tests determined that Cucich had been given a shot of Pavulon, a muscle relaxant used in surgery when a tube is inserted in an anaesthetized patient. It is also one of the three drugs administered in a lethal injection in some states where that is permitted. In the right quantity it causes muscle paralysis, leading to suffocation. Anectine, another muscle relaxant, was also found. Neither drugs had been prescribed to Cucich.

On 13 November, the police searched Angelo's hospital locker and found a hypodermic needle and a vial of potassium chloride, another of the drugs used in lethal injection which causes cardiac arrest. The following day they searched his apartment, finding vials of Pavulon and Anectine. Angelo was arrested on 16 November.

Neighbours in Lindenhurst were both shocked and fascinated by his arrest. The newspapers sold out by 10 a.m.

'He was the guy next door,' said one. 'He was a quiet person who kept himself to himself.'

Because he worked nights they rarely saw him. When they did, it was only to nod and say hello. A neighbour who lived down the block from his childhood home said the family was cordial but something of an enigma.

'The family was a nice family and the boy was a nice boy, but very few people knew them well enough,' she said. 'They had a Cape Cod house that they always kept immaculate.'

Daniel P. Walsh, president of the Good Samaritan Hospital said: 'He was good in a crisis. This guy had all the credentials. But he seemed a little on edge the last couple of weeks.'

A spokesman for the hospital said: 'The people in the emergency room – the doctors and the nurses – they spoke highly of him.'

In his free time, Angelo volunteered as an emergency medical technician with the Lindenhurst Volunteer Fire Department and taught technician courses in Suffolk County.

'Most of his acquaintances were nurses and paramedics – this was his life,' said Sergeant Alfred T. Anderson of the State University police at Farmingdale, who had taken an emergency medical technician recertification course with Angelo the previous year.

Once in custody, Angelo confessed to a series of murders, saying he had injected two patients with Pavulon or Anective during September and early October. He hadn't intended to kill them. His aim was to push them to the brink of death, then step in and save them, making himself a hero in the eyes of his colleagues and those whose lives he had saved. However, his plan had a fatal flaw and many of his victims died.

In a taped interview, Angelo said: 'I wanted to create a situation where I would cause the patient to have some respiratory distress or some problem, and through my intervention or suggested intervention or whatever, come out looking like I knew what I was doing. I had no confidence in myself. I felt very inadequate.'

In Angelo's last six weeks on the job, there were 37 'Code Blue' emergencies on his ward, with a loss of 25 patients. The other 12 lived to speak of their near-death experiences.

The bodies of those who had died on the ward were exhumed and examined. Deadly drugs were found in ten former patients. Prosecutors were conservative in their estimate, saying only that the number Angelo's victims was 'in excess of ten'. Other published reports placed the body-count as high as 38. A legal technicality prevented Angelo's confession being used in the courtroom. So, for the moment, only one charge of first-degree assault was filed. This was for the attack on Girolamo Cucich. Angelo was granted bail with a surety of $50,000 provided he stayed in Suffolk County, but he chose to stay in custody out of fear for his safety.

'Richard's not coming out,' Angelo's attorney Eric Nalburg told the newspapers. 'People will recognize him.... They'll yell things at him. I want a client with a clear head as we prepare for the case.'

He had also received letters threatening his life.

The head of Suffolk County homicide bureau said: 'We have an excellent case of assault against Angelo.' But when it came to murder charges, he said that they were still waiting for the result of tests to determine if drugs caused the deaths of any patients.

By mid-December, laboratory tests had been completed on 19 corpses. On 4 January 1988, it was announced that two patients, Milton Poulney and Frederick LaGois, had each been injected with Pavulon prior to death. Anectine could not be detected as it disappears in the body after 24 hours. On 13 January, charges of second-degree murder were filed against Angelo in the LaGois case. More indictments followed.

Mental-health defence

Angelo's lawyers sought to advance a mental-health defence. Two psychologists testified that he suffered from a personality disorder called dissociative identity disorder, formerly known as multiple personality disorder. The defence argued that Angelo did not realize the risk he was putting his patients in and, after he'd injected them, he had moved into a separate personality that made him unaware of what he had just done.

This theory was backed up by the fact that Angelo had been wired to a polygraph during questioning, which indicated he was being truthful about what he said about his state of mind during the murders. However, the judge would not allow the polygraph evidence to be used in court.

Countering this, the state had two mental health experts who agreed that Angelo suffered from a personality disorder, but not one that precluded him from appreciating whether his actions were right or wrong, or even just risky. The prosecution argued that he knew exactly what he was doing while he was doing it.

After eight days' deliberation, the jury convicted Angelo of two counts of second-degree murder, one count of second-degree manslaughter, one count of criminally negligent homicide, and six counts of assault. Urging the judge to impose the maximum sentence, the prosecutor John Collins said: 'Angelo truly was a monster.' And he asked the court to treat Angelo with the same lack of compassion that he showed his victims.

'These were no folks who took an ill-advised stroll in Central Park after dark,' he said. 'These were sick, vulnerable people who had entrusted their care to the defendant.'

Imposing the maximum allowable sentence, Judge Alfred Tisch said: 'You have no right to usurp God's function.' Angelo showed no emotion, while Judge Tisch went on to say that Angelo had violated 'in the cruellest, most inhumane manner' the childlike trust hospital patients placed in a nurse. The patients, most of them sick and elderly, 'had a right to enjoy, in their own way, every day that was available to them,' the judge said.

Angelo did not speak at the hearing. He was sentenced to 61 years to life. The sentence included two terms of 25 years for murder and sentences ranging from 16 months to four years on the counts of criminally negligent homicide. Because the murder terms were to be served consecutively, Angelo would not be eligible for parole for 50 years. He was sent to the notorious Clinton Correctional Facility in Dannemora, upstate New York. He was just 27. His attorney Eric Nalby said he would lodge an appeal, though he had expected the maximum sentence. Outside the courthouse, some of the victims' family members said they wished Angelo had been given the death sentence, but it was not available in New York state at the time.

The Good Samaritan Hospital came in for criticism, with the New York state Health Department concluding that 'shortcomings in the hospital's quality assurance system rendered the facility unable to detect potential patient care problems such as the maladministration of medications'. The hospital's president Daniel P. Walsh responded after a three-hour meeting of the board of trustees: 'We are being painted with a very broad brush, and it is very frustrating for many of us at the hospital. We still think we run a quality hospital.'

The hospital was also cited for 'inadequate patient care monitoring' and poor record keeping.

THE LAINZ ANGELS OF DEATH: WALTRAUD WAGNER, MARIA GRUBER, IRENE LEIDOLF AND STEPHANIJA MAYER

Humane killing

In Lainz General Hospital in Vienna four nurses murdered as many as two hundred elderly and infirm patients who annoyed them. Allitt's murderous spree went on for a matter of weeks, but the Lainz Angels of Death managed to stay under the radar for six years.

In 1982, 23-year-old Waltraud Wagner began work as a nurse's aide at Lainz General Hospital's Pavilion Five, which housed elderly patients, many of whom were terminally ill. Initially, she sought to make her patients comfortable and ease their pain and suffering, then in the spring of 1983 a 70-year-old woman patient repeatedly begged Wagner to put her out of her misery. Wagner refused, but while she was off duty she reflected on the woman's appeals.

Plainly her death was inevitable, for no one recovered in Pavilion Five, and Wagner began to think that perhaps it was more humane to accede to the patient's request. So the next time the old woman begged for death Wagner gave her an overdose of morphine and watched the pained expression on her face turn to one of bliss.

Wagner had no regrets about what she had done. She was pleased that she had relieved someone whose life had run its course and when other patients begged her to end their suffering she obliged. Soon she got used to playing God.

Over the years, Wagner was joined on the graveyard shift in Pavilion Five by 19-year-old Maria Gruber, a single mother and nursing-school dropout, and 21-year-old Irene Leidolf, who had a husband at home but preferred hanging out with the other women after work. Like Wagner, they came from large families in rural Austria with little higher education. While drinking in a bar near the hospital it was natural for them to discuss their patients and Wagner suggested to them that, in some cases, patients should be put out of their misery. It was the compassionate thing to do. The other two agreed. It upset them to see their patients suffering so much.

Wagner taught them how to administer the right amount of morphine that would be lethal but not arouse suspicion. They saw this as mercy killing and felt no guilt. Later the deadly team was completed by Stephanija Mayer, a divorced grandmother who had emigrated from Yugoslavia. She was 20 years older than Wagner but despite her seeming maturity she was happy to go along with the terminal procedures the others had established.

'The water cure'

Until 1987 they despatched only the most severely ill, but then the termination rate accelerated. They began to kill any patient they found annoying. These included patients who made a complaint, summoned the nurse during the night, snored loudly, soiled the sheets or refused their medication. These minor infractions would result in a death sentence, with Wagner joking that the patient concerned had booked 'a ticket to God' or had 'a meeting with the undertaker'.

To avoid questions about the amount of morphine that was being used, they began to despatch patients using insulin and Rohypnol. Then to cover their tracks more completely, Wagner introduced what she called 'the water cure'. Patients' heads would be tipped back, with their tongues depressed and their nostrils pinched, and then a jug full of water would be poured down their throats, filling their lungs. They would then drown. It was a slow and agonizing death, though virtually undetectable. Elderly patients frequently had fluid in their lungs when they died and the killing went on unimpeded.

Nurses laugh about killings

By 1988, rumours were rife that a murderer was at work in Pavilion Five, but the head of the ward Dr Franz Xavier Pesendorfer made no effort to investigate. The Angels of Death were eventually betrayed by their own hubris. In February 1989, while having a drink after work, they were discussing the death of elderly patient Julia Drapal. She had been given the water cure for refusing her medication and calling Wagner a slut, so clearly she deserved to die. A doctor seated nearby heard them laughing about it and reported the matter to the police. The four women were suspended while the bodies of those who had died on the ward were exhumed. Many were found with water in their lungs, which proved nothing, but others were found with high levels of morphine, insulin or Rohypnol in their bodies. After a six-week investigation, Wagner, Gruber, Leidolf and Mayer were arrested and charged with murder.

In court: (from left to right) Stephanija Mayer, Maria Gruber, Irene Leidolf and Waltraud Wagner. They claimed they had killed elderly parents out of pity, but did they enjoy their power too much?

Like Nazi euthanasia programme

News of the killings stunned Austria. They brought to mind Nazi medical experiments at Auschwitz and other Nazi death camps. The mayor of Vienna called the four nurses the 'death angels'. They were seen as sadists, like the women who had guarded the concentration camps, which were still fresh in the memory of many Austrians.

Between them, the four women admitted killing 49 patients who were too demanding or troublesome. Wagner alone admitted 39 murders. But later they retracted substantial parts of their confessions, claiming that they had killed only a handful of patients who were terminally ill, to alleviate their pain. Wagner admitted only ten assisted deaths and they were mercy killings, she insisted.

More bodies were exhumed and they were charged with the 42 counts of murder. However, the state prosecutor said that the number of victims was much higher and would probably never be known. Some estimates put the number as high as 200.

In the month-long trial, the state prosecutor Ernst Kloyber evoked Austria's Nazi past. He told the jury:

> This was no mercy killing, but cold-blooded murder of helpless people, which reminds us of a period in Austrian history none of us likes to remember ... It is a small step from killing the terminally ill to the killing of insolent, burdensome patients, and from there to what was known under the Third Reich as euthanasia. It is a door that must never be opened again.

The judge dismissed Wagner's claim that they were alleviating pain, pointing to her use of the 'water cure'.

'These patients were gasping for breath for up to half a day before they died,' he said. 'You cannot call that pain relief.'

Wagner was convicted of 15 counts of murder, 17 counts of attempted murder and two counts of physical assault. She was sentenced to life imprisonment. Leidolf was convicted of five murders and also sentenced to life. Both immediately appealed. Mayer was sentenced to 20 years and Gruber to 15 for manslaughter and attempted murder. It had been the biggest murder trial in Austria since World War II.

Youth culture blamed

Dr Pesendorfer had been suspended when the four nurses were arrested in April 1989 and he was found culpable of failing to pursue rumours of mass killings in his department that had been circulating for at least a year. He defended his actions, saying he had alerted the authorities, doctors and supervisory nurses and had ordered post-mortems as soon as suspicions were raised.

'What more could I have done?' he said. 'The dead were not

victims of the system but victims of crimes that could not have been anticipated and prevented.'

Other criticisms were levelled at the health service. Hildegard Fach, the head of the National Union of Nurses, said that the four women were merely nurses' aides and were not qualified to give injections. She said that regulations were routinely violated in Austrian hospitals, with nurses' aides allowed to give medication intravenously when their duties were supposed to be limited to cleaning, feeding and assisting patients. As a result, innocent nurses had been abused by the public. One even said she had been spat upon.

Commentators pointed out that the case spoke volumes about post-war society, which had become increasingly obsessed with youth and material wellbeing at the expense of any sensitivity towards the aged and infirm. A survey showed that 25 per cent of those questioned thought that euthanasia was justifiable in some circumstances.

A front-page editorial in the Viennese newspaper *Die Presse* said:

> The most recent investigation into what is 'holy' to the Austrians showed it quite clearly: Their own health is most important to the individual, but the general protection of human life – in the narrow, as well as the broadest sense – ranked behind protecting material goods. To damage an auto appears to be much worse than visiting injustice or harm on one's fellow man.

Given new identities

Gruber and Mayer, convicted on lesser charges, were discreetly released in the 1990s and given new identities by the Austrian government, but in 2008 the release of Wagner and Leidolf caused outrage. The Austrian newspaper *Heute* carried the headline: 'The death angels are getting out.'

Even before their release, they had been let out to go shopping or visit the hairdressers. It was explained that this was part of a pre-release programme preparing them for life outside prison. They would have been released soon anyway, as in Austria those sentenced to life only serve 15 years. They too were given new identities, so they could resume life anonymously.

'It's inhumane and immoral to execute a killer,' said one Viennese citizen, 'but it's not fair to their victims' loved ones when a killer can look forward to a nice life outside prison.'

BEVERLEY ALLITT

First mysterious death

On 23 February 1991, just two days after Beverley Allitt had started work as a nurse on Children's Ward Four at Grantham and Kesteven Hospital in Lincolnshire, seven-week-old Liam Taylor was brought in with a chest infection.

His doctor did not think his condition was serious but in hospital it could be properly monitored. The staff nurse said that newly enrolled state nurse Allitt would take good care of him, but when they returned two hours later they were told that he had taken a turn for the worse.

'I was feeding him and he suddenly threw up,' said Allitt. 'It went all over me. I had to go and change my uniform.'

The child was so sick, she said, that he had stopped breathing for a moment.

'He was choking on his vomit,' she said. 'If he'd been at home, you'd probably have lost him.'

The couple were upset but took an instant liking to the young nurse who was so frank with them and they were relieved and grateful when Allitt volunteered for an extra night shift to look after him. However, early in the morning Allitt called for an emergency resuscitation team as Liam had stopped breathing. The doctors managed to revive him, but there was bad news. The specialist told Liam's parents that, if their child survived, he would have severe brain damage.

'Normally, in children who have respiratory failure, their condition can be stabilized in a matter of minutes,' Dr Charith Nanayakkara said. 'In Liam's case, it took an hour and fifteen minutes.'

The chaplain was called to christen the child. Liam's parents then agreed to switch off the life support system, but Liam did not die – not immediately anyway. His parents took turns holding him until he finally perished seven and a half hours later.

The doctors could not understand how he had died. A post-mortem concluded that Liam had suffered an 'infarction' of the heart – that is, the muscles of the heart had died. This usually happened in patients in middle age or beyond, after a lifetime of heavy smoking or drinking, so the pathologist could not explain how it had happened to a tiny child.

Insulin in blood

Then on 5 March, just three days after Liam had been buried, 11-year-old Timothy Hardwick was admitted to Ward Four. He had been born with cerebral palsy and had suffered an epileptic fit. Again Allitt seemed to lavish care on the child and initially the doctors were pleased with his progress. Suddenly, when the ward was particularly busy, Timothy unexpectedly died. Given his chronic condition, no further investigation was made and no one called the police.

In the same bed just five days later, 14-month-old Kayley Desmond stopped breathing while in the care of Allitt. Then her heart stopped beating. She was revived and rushed to the intensive care unit at the Queen's Medical Centre in Nottingham, amid concern that she might have suffered brain damage when starved of oxygen. It was assumed that this had occurred when, as a bad feeder, she had inhaled milk and stopped breathing. No one spotted that under her right armpit there was a needle puncture with a small bubble of air behind it, as if

Beverley Allitt had been to Grantham College of Further Education with Sue Phillips. Allitt told Phillips she would look after her daughter Katie. 'She will be alright with me.'

someone had injected her ineptly. It was only seen when her X-rays were re-examined later. Nevertheless, Kayley made a full recovery.

Another ten days passed before five-month-old Paul Crampton was admitted to the ward with mild bronchitis. Responding well to treatment, he was due to be discharged four days later when suddenly he took a turn for the worse.

Sue Phillips, the mother of Becky and Katie Phillips, who were also on the ward, said: 'I heard Bev Allitt say: "I think I know what's wrong with him. He's hypoglycaemic."'

Paul was put on a glucose drip and quickly recovered.

'I thought how clever the nurse was to have realized what was wrong with him so quickly,' Sue Phillips said.

He had two more unexplained attacks of hypoglycaemia, a critical lack of sugar in his body. After the third attack, he was rushed to the Queen's Medical Centre, with Allitt in the ambulance, where the lab discovered that he had a high level of insulin in his blood.

Parents' gratitude

The following day five-year-old Bradley Gibson was admitted suffering from pneumonia and during the night he complained of pain in the arm where his antibiotic drip was attached. He was attended by Allitt. On the second occasion, he suffered a cardiac arrest. For half an hour, the emergency resuscitation team battled to save him – successfully – and he too was taken to the Queen's. His parents went to the local newspaper, the *Grantham Journal*, to praise the doctors and nurses who had saved their son and the paper ran the story under the headline 'Our Miracle'. Three national newspapers picked up on it.

The day after that, two-year-old Yik Hung 'Henry' Chan was admitted after he had plunged from a bedroom window on to the patio below, suffering a fractured skull. Although he was dizzy and complaining of bad headaches, his condition quickly improved and the doctors were thinking about sending him home. However, when attended by

Allitt the child started vomiting. Other staff saw he was blue, so the emergency team were called and he was revived with oxygen. When this happened a second time, Henry, too, was rushed to the Queen's.

Four days later, it was the turn of identical twins Becky and Katie Phillips. Becky had been admitted for observation after suffering from acute gastroenteritis. She was untroubled for the first two days because Allitt had been off duty. When she returned, Becky's mother Sue Phillips recognized her immediately, because they had been to Grantham College of Further Education together. Strangely, though, Allitt did not acknowledge her.

When Becky returned home she fell ill again and was taken back to hospital. The doctors suspected that the problem was with the milk the twins were being fed. Whereas the hospital used ready-mixed baby's milk, Sue mixed her own from powder. That evening Becky screamed and her eyes rolled in her head. Allitt did not want Sue to take Becky home but nevertheless she was discharged. However, despite a midnight rush to A&E, she died in the night. No reason could be found, though the doctor in A&E thought she might have contracted meningitis. The death certificate said 'infant death syndrome' – cot death.

As a precaution, Katie was sent to hospital for observation, only to be cared for by Allitt, who now offered Sue seemingly genuine words of comfort. Seeing Sue was tired, Allitt told her to go home and get some rest.

'You go. I will look after her,' said Allitt. 'She will be all right with me.'

Within half an hour of reaching home, Sue got a call saying Katie was having trouble breathing. She suffered a cardiac arrest, but Allitt was on hand to call for 'resus'. Emergency treatment saved Katie's life, but the same thing happened again two days later. Rushed to the Queen's, she was found to have suffered brain damage. She had cerebral palsy, paralysis of the right side and damage to her eyesight and hearing. What's more, five of her ribs were broken. This was put down to frantic efforts to resuscitate her. But Katie's mother Sue was so grateful to Allitt for saving her daughter's life that she asked her to be her godmother. As it was, the hospital's chaplain became Katie's godparent.

Questions raised

A few days later, six-year-old Michael Davidson was admitted after being accidentally shot with an airgun. After minor surgery to remove the pellet, Allitt helped prepare an intravenous antibiotic. When it was administered, the child stopped breathing. His face turned black and his back arched. CPR from Dr Nanayakkara had him breathing again before the emergency team arrived and after being resuscitated he recovered and was eventually discharged.

That same day two-month-old Christopher Peasgood was admitted with breathing difficulties. While he was put in an oxygen tent, Allitt suggested that his parents, who had lost a child to cot death two years earlier, should go and have a cup of tea. When they returned they found the emergency team in action. The boy was blue. A nurse had discovered that the alarm indicating he had stopped breathing had been turned off. Nevertheless, Allitt assured Christopher's parents that he would be alright, but he suffered another cardiac arrest during the night. Fearing that he was dying, the child was christened. The doctors wanted to send him to the Queen's but feared he might not survive the journey. However, Christopher's parents agreed to the move, figuring they had nothing to lose, and in the intensive care unit there he quickly recovered.

Christopher King was a month old when he was admitted for an operation, but he became inexplicably ill before going to surgery and had to be revived with oxygen. The operation was a success, but he had to be resuscitated four more times before he was sent to the Queen's. His mother Belinda was a nurse and she swore that she would never take Christopher back to Ward Four.

Seven-week-old Patrick Elstone had been playing and laughing when his parents had dropped him off for a check-up, but in Allitt's care he had stopped breathing – twice. He was rushed to the Queen's, but not before he had suffered brain damage. By then, the doctors at the Queen's were beginning to ask the question: Why were so many children coming into their care from Ward Four?

Lignocaine found

Asthmatic 15-month-old Claire Peck had been admitted to the ward on 18 April. She was put on a nebulizer that cleared her airways and she was discharged two days later, but after a coughing fit she returned on 22 April. Her mother Susan found Nurse Allitt unfriendly, even hostile, and the Pecks had been ushered away while their daughter was being treated. Left alone with the child, Allitt suddenly cried out: 'Arrest! Arrest!'

Doctors came running and revived the child, but as soon as she was left alone with Allitt the same thing happened again. This time the doctors could not save her. Susan Peck, holding the dead child, noticed that everyone else was upset but Allitt just sat there staring.

The authorities at first suspected that legionnaires' disease was responsible, so although no virus was found the ward was meticulously scrubbed. Initially a post-mortem showed that Claire had died from natural causes, but Dr Nelson Porter, a consultant at the hospital, was unhappy with the number of heart cases that had occurred in Ward Four over the previous eight weeks and ordered further tests. Lignocaine, a drug that was used to treat adults suffering from cardiac arrest, was found in Claire's body. It was never given to babies.

The police were called in and it was discovered, by checking the rotas, that Allitt was the only person who was present every time there was a medical emergency. Also, notes covering Paul Crampton's stay were missing. Allitt was suspended, but the parents of the Phillips twins had so much faith in her that they hired a private detective to clear her name.

Munchausen's Syndrome

After Allitt's arrest a missing ward diary was found in her home. She was charged with four counts of murder and 11 counts of attempted murder, to which she pleaded not guilty at Nottingham Crown Court on 15 February 1993. In the court case, which lasted two months, the prosecution easily showed that Allitt had the means and the opportunity to commit the crimes – but what of the motive? Consultant paediatrician Professor Roy Meadow told the court that Allitt exhibited all the symptoms of Munchausen's Syndrome and Munchausen's Syndrome by Proxy. In the first condition, the sufferer seeks attention by self-harm or faking complaints. Allitt's extensive medical record confirmed that. Even while she had been out on bail she had been admitted to hospital complaining of an enlarged right breast. It was discovered that she had been injecting herself with water. She attended the court for just 16 days, absenting herself for the rest of the time due to mysterious illnesses.

The second condition is usually exhibited by mothers, where they seek medical attention by complaining that their offspring is suffering from fictitious complaints or by inflicting actual abuse. Professor Meadow said that to suffer from both Munchausen's Syndrome and Munchausen's Syndrome by Proxy was extremely rare, but he came across around 40 cases of the proxy condition a year.

Allitt was found guilty on all charges. In Children's Ward Four at Grantham and Kesteven Hospital in Lincolnshire, she had administered potentially lethal injections or attempted to suffocate 23 children in her charge, killing four and leaving a further nine irreparably damaged – all in just 59 days.

Danger signs since childhood

In court, it became clear that Beverley Allitt should never have been allowed to become a nurse because she had shown disturbing symptoms of a mental disorder from an early age. One of four children, she sought attention by wearing dressings and casts over supposed wounds that she would allow no one to examine. Growing overweight as an adolescent, her attention-seeking became aggressive and her parents regularly had to take her to hospital for treatment for fictitious ailments. These included pain in her gall bladder, headaches, urinary infections, uncontrolled vomiting, blurred vision, minor injuries, back trouble, ulcers and appendicitis, resulting in the removal of a perfectly healthy appendix. The scar was slow to heal as she kept picking at the wound.

While training as a nurse she had a poor attendance record, frequently being absent with supposed illnesses. She was also suspected of odd behaviour, including smearing faeces on the walls of the nurses' home. Her boyfriend accused her of being aggressive, manipulative and deceptive. She falsely claimed to be pregnant and told people he had AIDS and she had accused a friend of his of rape, though she did not go to the police.

When Allitt returned to the dock for sentencing, the judge told her:

> You have been found guilty of the most terrible crimes. You killed, tried to kill or seriously harmed thirteen children, many of them tiny babies. They had been entrusted to your care. You have brought grief to their families. You have sown a seed of doubt in those who should have faith in the integrity of care their children receive in hospital. Hopefully, the grief felt by the families will become easier to bear, but it will always be there. You are seriously disturbed. You are cunning and manipulative and you have shown no remorse for the trail of destruction you have left behind you. I accept it is all the result of the severe personality disorder you have. But you are and remain a very serious danger to others.

He gave her 13 concurrent terms of life imprisonment, which meant she would serve a minimum of 30 years and would only be released if she was considered to be no danger to the public. Committed to Rampton Secure Hospital, she admitted three of the murders and six of the attempted murders. Her earliest possible parole date is 2032, when she will be 64. Meanwhile, the families and the victims whom she disabled will have to live a lifetime with what she has done.

DOROTHEA PUENTE

orothea Puente ran the prettiest of boarding houses in Sacramento, California. The two-storey gingerbread Victorian house was situated at 1426 F Street, a lush, tree-lined thoroughfare in what had once been a grand neighbourhood. Dorothea's house stood out proudly from the others, which had fallen into disrepair. She took great pride in the look of her home. It was decorated with lace doilies and a variety of knick-knacks. The 59-year-old Dorothea also paid a great deal of attention to her own appearance. She spent a sizeable amount of money on silk chiffon dresses, Giorgio Armani perfume and at least one facelift.

Prim and proper
Dorothea lived an orderly life, which was reflected in her orderly boarding house. Boarders lived on the ground floor, while Dorothea had the spacious second floor to herself. It was all quite proper. Her guests paid $350 per month. In exchange they received a private room and two very generous meals each day. If there was anything amiss it was the foul stench that appeared to be coming from her property. During the summer months the neighbours would complain to Dorothea. She would then come up with all sorts of excuses: the

sewer was blocked up; rats were to blame; she had been using a fish emulsion to fertilize her back garden.

She tried to eliminate the smell, or at least cover it up, by dumping a quantity of lime and gallon after gallon of bleach on to her back garden. The boarding house itself was sprayed constantly with air freshener. When three police officers came to call on the morning of 11 November 1988, she had perhaps already sprayed her house. They were looking for one of her boarders, a 51-year-old mentally disabled man named Alvaro Montoya. It was not that Alvaro was in trouble with the law – he just seemed to have vanished. His social worker was most concerned.

While Alvaro's room did not provide any clues as to his whereabouts, the officers noticed something unusual in Dorothea's back garden. In one corner of the property it appeared that the ground had been recently disturbed. Using shovels and spades, the three men began digging. Finally, they uncovered clothing and the remains of a human body. No one expressed more shock at the discovery than Dorothea.

Officials from the coroner's office arrived, as did a team of forensic anthropologists, supported by a work crew. Together, they worked to uncover the corpse. It appeared that the police officers had found the skeleton of a short female with grey hair. But that wasn't all. As the excavation continued, a second set of remains was uncovered – and these were much fresher.

More cadavers

Just after this gruesome discovery had been made, Dorothea asked the detective in charge, John Cabrera, whether she might be permitted to go for coffee at the Clarion Hotel, just two blocks away. There was no problem with this request. After all, the boarding house owner was not under arrest. The detective did Dorothea the courtesy of escorting her through the gathered onlookers and then he returned to the garden.

As the afternoon progressed, the body count increased. Three more cadavers were found underneath a slab of concrete and another body had been buried beneath a gazebo. In the end, seven corpses – three male and four female – were found in Dorothea's back garden.

It went without saying that Dorothea would have to be questioned about the bodies that had been unearthed on her property. The only problem was that Dorothea had disappeared. She had never returned from her trip to the Clarion Hotel. Despite Dorothea's absence, a picture began to emerge. A note found in her quarters served as the key to what had been taking place. On this small piece of paper was written Alvaro's first initial, followed by those of six former boarders. Each of the initials was accompanied by a number, which was preceded by a dollar sign. The investigators had found a list of Social Security and disability benefits. Dorothea had been collecting money that had been intended for people who were dead. She became richer by $5,000 each and every month.

As they searched for the boarding house owner, the authorities began looking into her background. What they found was not pretty. She had been born Dorothea Helen Gray in Redlands, California, on 9 January 1929. Both of her parents had died by the time she was nine – her mother in a horrible motorcycle accident – and she was sent to a number of homes. As a teenager, she turned to prostitution. She was able to earn a fair amount of money from her good looks.

Unhappy union

Not long after the end of World War II, Dorothea met a 22-year-old soldier named Fred McFaul. They married in Reno. Though the couple had two daughters, their union was not a happy one. Dorothea lived an unrealistic fantasy life that required expensive clothing and evenings out.

She told people that she was the sister of the American ambassador to Sweden and that she counted Rita Hayworth among her closest friends.

Dorothea Puente invented a variety of excuses to explain the foul stench that came from her property.

In the midst of this fantasy life, she left her husband and daughters for the excitement of Los Angeles. There she became pregnant by another man. Though she miscarried, McFaul would not take her back. With the marriage at an end, their children were raised by others. Then in 1948, Dorothea served her first jail sentence. She was locked up for a total of four years after forging a number of cheques. Almost as soon as she was released, Dorothea wed for a second time. Though the marriage lasted for some 14 years, it was another disaster. It is likely that it only endured as long as it did because her husband, a merchant seaman, was often away.

Dorothea carried on working as a prostitute during both her marriages and in 1960 she was convicted of residing in a brothel. In 1968, she married for a third time. Her groom, Robert Jose Puente, was just over half Dorothea's age. A year later, the marriage was over. As the 1970s began, Dorothea started to run the boarding house on F Street. After a few years, she ended up marrying one of her boarders, a 52-year-old named Pedro Angel Montalvo. The couple had not been married long when Dorothea was again arrested for cheque forgery. This time she avoided prison. She got away with five years' probation for the crime.

It is thought by the authorities that she committed her first murder in 1982. The victim, Ruth Munroe, made the mistake of starting a small lunchroom business with Dorothea. This happy, optimistic woman died from an overdose of codeine and Tylenol, a tragedy that the coroner dismissed as suicide. A mere month later, Dorothea was charged with drugging her boarders so that she could steal their more pricey possessions. It was a simple and obvious crime. As a result, she served three years in the California Institution for Women. Upon her release, Dorothea was told not to handle government cheques and to keep away from senior citizens. She violated both orders.

Still officially married to her fourth husband, the 56-year-old Dorothea became engaged to Everson Gillmouth, a man 21 years her senior. His body was found a few months later by fishermen who had been trying their luck in the Sacramento River.

Attracting custom

By this point, Dorothea had returned to running her boarding house. A string of social workers favoured her with boarders. They were oblivious to her lengthy criminal record. In the words of one of their number, Dorothea had the 'best the system had to offer'. She was willing to accept into her boarding house the most difficult people that they had to place. However, she did not rely entirely on social workers for boarders. Dressed to the nines, Dorothea frequented the lesser bars of Sacramento. There she made conversation with lonely, down-and-out people, in a bid to encourage them to take a room at her boarding house.

All of these revelations came much too late. By November 1988 the authorities knew that they had to find Dorothea. But where was she?

Bogus story

The investigators were later able to piece together just what had happened. After Detective Cabrera had escorted her to the Clarion Hotel, Dorothea had spent some time in a bar on the other side of town. She had then boarded a bus for Los Angeles, where she had met a 59-year-old carpenter named Charles Willgues in a tavern. She gave him a fake name and an equally bogus story – a cab driver had driven off with her suitcases. Dorothea tried to play upon the man's sympathy, but she did not get very far. When she suggested that they move in together, the carpenter declined. Later, in his apartment, Charles realized the true identity of the woman to whom he had been speaking. It was then that he called the police.

She was arrested the day after the bodies began to be pulled out of the ground. The former prostitute was later charged with nine counts of murder. It would take four years before Dorothea's case was ready to go to trial.

Her defence was extremely weak. Dorothea explained that the people whose bodies had been found in her back garden had all died of natural causes. She had buried them herself in order to hide the fact that she was operating a boarding house in violation of her parole. However, Dorothea's claims about natural deaths were countered by the concentrations of Dalmane, a prescription-strength sleeping pill, that were present in every one of the remains.

A friend of Alvaro Montoya took the stand to say that the dead man had complained that Dorothea had been plying him with drugs. The testimony of other witnesses indicated that the boarding house owner had been forcing drugs on her lodgers.

Dorothea was eventually found guilty on three counts of murder.

On 10 December 1993, she was sentenced to life imprisonment without the possibility of parole. She died in prison in 2011, at the age of 82.

WANETA HOYT

Mrs Waneta Hoyt seemed to have been the unluckiest of mothers. Five of her children died of sudden infant death syndrome (SIDS), also known as cot or crib death. This is a catchall term for the unexplained death of an infant. However, in the 1960s and 1970s, there were attempts to discover the causes and give the syndrome some medical credibility.

Waneta Nixon was born in Richford, New York, in 1946. At 11, she caught measles which left her with poor eyesight, only seeing shadows without her glasses. At 17, she married Tim Hoyt, who worked as a Pinkerton guard at Cornell University's art museum 32 km (20 miles) away at Ithaca.

After nine months she gave birth to a son named Eric. He died three months later, on 26 January 1965. The following year she gave birth to James. Their daughter Julie was born in 1968. She died after seven weeks. James was two years old when he died suddenly, too. A grief-stricken Waneta sought help from a psychiatrist, but quit attending after five months. Three months later, the Hoyts filled out an application at the county's social service agency to adopt a child. But that summer Waneta fell pregnant again and dropped her plans to adopt.

The following March their daughter Molly was born. Fearing that she might also succumb to cot death, the Hoyts took her to the Upstate Medical Center to see Dr Alfred Steinschneider, an expert on sleep apnoea – that is, the sudden cessation of breathing thought to be the cause of SIDS. Molly Hoyt became the first baby in the United States to be sent home on an apnoea monitor. But after just two days, Waneta called Dr Steinschneider because Molly had experienced another spell and she'd had to resuscitate her. Steinschneider told her to bring Molly back to Upstate Medical Center and he readmitted the child. Soon, Molly was discharged and sent home again with the apnoea monitor. The following day, she died. She was two-and-a-half months old.

A week later, the Hoyts made another application to adopt, but this fell through when the caseworker discovered that Waneta was pregnant again. Their fifth child, Noah, was born on 9 May 1971. He was also admitted to the Upstate Medical Center for evaluation. After a month he was discharged. Within three days, Noah was back at Upstate Medical Center. Waneta said Noah had stopped breathing and she'd had to resuscitate him.

On 27 July 1971, he was discharged again. He died the following day. He was two-and-a-half months old. Meanwhile, Tim Hoyt had undergone a vasectomy, thinking that whatever was killing their children was hereditary, so they should not have any more.

A week after Noah died, the Hoyts applied to adopt a child again. On 19 November 1971, they took home a nine-month-old baby boy named Scottie on a six-month trial basis. After five days, Waneta went to see a psychiatrist, fearing that she might hurt Scottie. The psychiatrist suggested to Waneta that she admit herself into a hospital. She refused. Instead, the psychiatrist reluctantly prescribed the drugs Stelazine to treat anxiety and Elavil to relieve depression. The following day, Waneta called social services and asked them to come and pick up Scottie, saying she wanted to wait a year or two before adopting. She then became suicidal.

In October 1972 Dr Steinschneider published a controversial article in the journal *Pediatrics* proposing a connection between sleep apnoea and SIDS. It was based on a case study of a family that had suffered five cot deaths. This seemed to indicate an hereditary cause for sleep apnoea and SIDS. In line with common practice in academic publishing in the medical field, the family were referred to only by their initial H.

Waneta had a hysterectomy in 1973. Then it seems she was raped by a neighbour, though strangely she wanted to continue the relationship with the man. He refused.

The Hoyts finally adopted a two-month-old boy named Jay on 20 September 1976, this time successfully. It was another ten years before Waneta went to see a psychiatrist again, saying that Jay was getting on her nerves. She was supposed to return in two weeks for a second appointment but never showed up.

First suspicions

In 1985, a New York State prosecutor William Fitzpatrick was working on a murder case that had originally been diagnosed as SIDS and consulted Dr Linda Norton, a forensic pathologist from Dallas and an expert on SIDS. In the course of their conversation, Norton remarked: 'You know, you have a serial killer right there in Syracuse.'

She had read Dr Steinschneider's article and told Fitzpatrick the odds against five such cot deaths in one family were incalculably high. She also found it suspicious that the mother was always alone with the babies when they died.

Shortly afterwards, Fitzpatrick left the prosecutor's office, but in 1992 he was sworn in as district attorney and looked into the case again. He consulted forensic pathologist Dr Michael Baden, who concluded that the children had been murdered.

'They were all healthy children,' says Baden. 'They had no natural cause for death. The only reasonable cause is homicidal suffocation.'

Fitzpatrick began tracking down the H family and quickly found that the Hoyts fitted the bill to a T. Noah had been given an autopsy, so Fitzpatrick subpoenaed his medical records from the Upstate Medical Center.

'Several hundred sheets of paper came in, chronicling the life history of this young lad, Noah Hoyt. It was really so sad,' he said.

Asked about the fate of her children, Waneta Hoyt insisted: 'I didn't want want them to die. I wanted them to quieten down.'

'For some reason, I developed an emotional attachment to Noah, you know, reading a record of virtually every day in his life. He was going to end up like the other four babies. You wanted to just reach back in through the hands of time and protect him.'

He had breathing problems and sometimes turned blue. There was a similar pattern surrounding the deaths of the other children.

'They all happened while the child was in the exclusive control of the mother,' he noted.

Fitzpatrick was DA in Onondaga County. The Hoyts had moved to nearby Tioga County, so Fitzpatrick contacted the prosecutor there and the state police were called in. They investigated the Hoyts and found they had a clean record. For more than 25 years, each Memorial Day, Waneta would drive to the small cemetery beside her childhood home in Richford to lay flowers on the graves of her babies.

A mother's fatal embrace

In March 1994, New York State Trooper Bobby Bleck approached Waneta in the post office and asked her if she would help him in some research he was doing on SIDS. She agreed and accompanied him to the police station where she was questioned by three state troopers. Several observers, including Fitzpatrick, watched through a two-way mirror.

At first, she seemed unruffled when they reprised the details of the tragic deaths of her five children years earlier and continued to protest her innocence. Then after an hour, investigator Susan Mulvey took Waneta's hand and said they did not believe her. Fifteen minutes later she admitted killing all five of them.

'I didn't want them to die,' she told the police. 'I wanted them to quieten down.'

Of Eric's death, she said: 'He was crying at the time and I wanted him to stop. I held a pillow – it might have been a sofa throw pillow – over his face while I was sitting on the couch. I don't remember if he struggled or not, but he did bleed from the mouth and nose.'

Asked about Julie, she said: 'I held her nose and mouth into my shoulder until she stopped struggling.'

Of James, who was upset about his sister's death, she said: 'I was in the bathroom getting dressed and he wanted to come in. He came in... and I made him go out. He started crying, "Mommy, mommy." I wanted him to stop crying for me so I used a bath towel to smother him.'

Then there was Molly: 'She was just home from the hospital overnight and was crying in her crib. I used a pillow that was in the crib to smother her. After she was dead, I called Mom Hoyt [Tim's mother] and Dr Steinschneider.'

Finally, Noah: 'I held a baby pillow over his face until he was dead. I then called for Mom Hoyt and Dr Steinschneider. I remember it was a hot day in July.'

After her confession, she asked to see her husband and told him what she had said. He said he did not believe her and accused the police of putting words in her mouth. That was not so, she said. He told her he loved her and she continued to tell all to the police.

In her signed statement, she said she had seen counsellors and a psychiatrist.

'I feel that if I had got help from them, it would have prevented me from killing the rest of my children,' she said. 'I feel that I am a good person, but I know that I did wrong. I loved my children. I love my adopted son, Jay, and my husband. I feel the burden I have carried by keeping the secret of killing my children has been a tremendous punishment. I most definitely feel remorse and regret for my actions. I cannot go back and undo the wrong that I have done.'

Trial and conviction

Waneta Hoyt later recanted her confession and its validity was contested during her trial. Testifying for the defence, Dr Charles Ewing said: 'It is my conclusion that her statement to the police on that day was not made knowingly, and it was not made voluntarily.'

He diagnosed that Waneta Hoyt had dependent and avoidant personality disorders, and was particularly vulnerable to the tactics used during her interrogation. Dr David Barry, a psychiatrist hired by the prosecution, agreed that Hoyt had been manipulated by the police tactics. There was also speculation that she suffered from Munchausen's syndrome by proxy, a diagnosis not universally accepted in this case.

Four nurses testified at the trial, saying that Mrs Hoyt showed little interest in her babies.

'There was no bonding at all,' said Thelma Schneider. 'Most of us went to Dr Steinschneider and expressed our fears – we had a gut feeling that something was going on. Either he was in total denial or not being very objective.'

Ambulance worker Robert Vanek, who went to the Hoyt residence when Julie, James and Noah died, recalled being stunned by the coroner's conclusion that all had died of SIDS.

'I thought, three in a row? It bothered me,' he said.

Discounting the post-mortem diagnoses of SIDS, Baden said the children's bodies were examined not by dispassionate forensic pathologists but by the family physician.

'Doctors,' he said, 'don't want to think parents harm children.'

In his testimony Dr Steinschneider continued to insist that the last two children to die suffered severe episodes of apnoea causing the SIDS that he believed had killed them. However, in his 1972 article, he had also noted the Hoyts' emotional detachment.

'Both parents often would be found sitting by the crib and had to be urged to make physical contact with the baby. It was my impression that they feared becoming too attached emotionally... because they anticipated a tragic outcome,' he wrote.

At the end of the four-week trial, Tioga County prosecutor Robert Simpson said in his closing arguments: 'Five young people aren't here today because of her. They would have had families, jobs. But they don't get that opportunity because their mother couldn't stand their crying.'

Waneta's husband Tim stuck by her, saying that the police had twisted her description of the children's deaths to make it sound like a confession. They had worn her down.

'She was used like an old tyre,' he said.

Her adopted son Jay added: 'I love her, and she shouldn't be here. The system sucks.' She, too, remained adamant in court.

'God forgive all of you who done this to me,' she said. 'I didn't kill my babies. I never did nothing in my life, and now to have this happen?' She was convicted of all five murders. Handing down his sentence, Judge Vincent Sgueglia said: 'I only have one thing to say to you and that is to consider your sixth child.... Whatever you tell this court, your husband, your God, you owe it to that boy to tell him the truth.'

On 11 September 1995, she was sentenced to 75 years to life – 15 years for each murder, to be served consecutively – for what Judge Sgueglia described as a 'depraved indifference to human life'. As four deputies escorted her from the courtroom, Jay bowed his head and cried.

Observing Hoyt, aged beyond her 49 years, Fitzpatrick said: 'Despite the cruelty of her acts, you'd be less than human not to have some degree of sympathy for her.'

He was less than sympathetic towards Dr Steinschneider, though.

'How could a doctor not realize that Molly and Noah were in harm's way?' he said. 'I know it was two-and-a-half decades ago. But was he overly consumed with expounding on his theory or was he concerned with his patient?'

Waneta Hoyt died of pancreatic cancer in prison on 13 August 1998. She was formally exonerated under New York law because she died before her appeal could be heard.

HAROLD SHIPMAN

With a total of over 200 suspected murders to his name, Harold Shipman is the most prolific serial killer of modern times. His grisly tally of victims puts him well ahead of Pedro Lopez, the 'monster of the Andes', who was convicted of 57 murders in 1980. (Lopez claimed to have killed many more, but the exact number of deaths was never verified.) Until Shipman's crimes came to light, Lopez had the dubious distinction of topping the serial killer league; at present, however, it is a British family doctor, rather than a penniless Colombian vagrant, who has become the world's number one murderer.

Mother's favourite

The sorry tale begins in 1946, when Harold Frederick Shipman was born into a working-class family in Nottingham. Known as Fred, the boy had an unusual childhood. He had a brother and sister, but it was clear that he was his mother's favourite. She felt that Fred was destined for great things, and taught him that he was superior to his contemporaries, even though he was not especially clever and had to work hard to achieve academic success. During his schooldays, he formed few friendships with other children, a situation that was exacerbated when his mother became seriously ill with lung cancer. The young Shipman took on the role of carer to his mother, spending time with her after school waiting for visits from the family doctor, who would inject her with morphine to relieve her from pain. It is possible that the stress of this experience during his formative years may have pushed him into mental illness, causing him to re-enact the role of carer and doctor in the macabre fashion that he later did.

By the time Shipman was 17, his mother had died of cancer, after a long and painful illness. He enrolled at medical school, despite having to resit his entry exams. Although he was good at sport, he made little effort to make friends. However, at this time he met and married his future wife Primrose; the pair went on to have four children, as Shipman began his career as a doctor in general practice. To many, he seemed kind and pleasant, but colleagues complained of his superior attitude and rudeness. Then he began to suffer from blackouts, which he attributed to epilepsy. However, disturbing evidence emerged that he was in fact taking large amounts of pethidine, on the pretext of prescribing the drug to patients. He was dismissed from the practice but, surprisingly, within two years he was once again working as a doctor, this time in a different town.

Pillar of the community

In his new job, the hard-working Shipman soon earned the respect of his colleagues and patients. However, it was during his time at Hyde, near Manchester, over a 24-year period, that he is estimated to have killed at least 236 patients. His status as a pillar of the community, not to mention his kindly bedside manner, for many years masked the fact that the death toll among Shipman's patients was astoundingly high.

Over the years a number of people, including relatives of the deceased and local undertakers, had raised concerns about the deaths of Shipman's patients. His victims always died suddenly, often with no previous record of terminal illness; and they were usually found sitting in a chair, fully clothed, rather than in bed. The police had been alerted and had examined the doctor's records, but nothing was found. It later became clear that Shipman had falsified patient records, but at this stage the doctor's calm air of authority was still protecting him against closer scrutiny.

Then Shipman made a fatal mistake. In 1998 Kathleen Grundy, a healthy, active 81-year-old ex-mayor with a reputation for community service, died suddenly at home. Shipman was called and pronounced her dead; he also said that a post-mortem was unnecessary, since he had paid her a visit shortly before her death. When her funeral was over, her daughter Angela Woodruff received a badly typed copy of Mrs Grundy's will leaving Shipman a large sum of money. A solicitor herself, Mrs Woodruff knew immediately that this was a fake. She contacted the police, who took the unusual step of exhuming Mrs Grundy's body. They found that she had been administered a lethal dose of morphine.

Surprisingly, in murdering Mrs Grundy, Shipman had made little effort to cover his tracks: either to forge the will carefully or to kill his victim with a less easily traceable drug. Whether this was through sheer arrogance and stupidity, or through a latent desire to be discovered, no one knows. However, once the true nature of Mrs Grundy's death was uncovered, more graves were opened, and more murders came to light.

During his trial, Shipman showed no remorse for the 15 murders he was accused of. (There were known to be others, but these alone were more than enough to ensure a life sentence.) He was contemptuous of the police and the court, and continued to protest his innocence to the end. He was convicted of the murders and imprisoned. Four years later, without warning, he hanged himself in his prison cell.

Today, the case of Harold Shipman remains mystifying: there was no sexual motive in his killings and, until the end, no profit motive. His murders did not fit the usual pattern of a serial killer. In most

Dr Harold Shipman, the most prolific serial killer in British history.

cases, his victims seem to have died in comfort, at peace. It may be, as several commentators have pointed out, that he enjoyed the sense of having control over life and death, and that over the years he became addicted to this sense of power. What is clear is that, in finally taking his own life, Harold Shipman ensured ultimate control: that no one would ever fully understand why he did what he did.

MICHAEL SWANGO

There were suspicions about Michael Swango from the start. Even when he was a medical student and given his first access to patients, classmates called him Double-O Swango, joking that he had a licence to kill. His attitude to the profession should have rung alarm bells. He enjoyed writing DIED in big red letters across the charts of recently deceased patients and once told a colleague that his job 'gives me an opportunity to come out of the emergency room with a hard-on to tell some parents that their kid has just died.'

As to his greatest fantasy, he told co-workers when was a paramedic with an ambulance crew: 'Picture a school bus crammed with kids smashing head-on with a trailer truck loaded down with gasoline. We're summoned. We get there in a jiffy just as another gasoline truck rams the bus. Up in flames it goes! Kids are hurled through the air, everywhere, on telephone poles, on the street, especially along an old barbed wire fence along the road. All burning.'

Despite this, other medical professionals simply overlooked the number of unexplained deaths among patients in his care. And he was regularly hired by hospitals even after he was a convicted poisoner.

Born in Tacoma, Washington, in 1954, Swango was largely raised in Quincy, Illinois. His father was a colonel in the Marine Corps, constantly on the move. After his second tour in Vietnam, he and Michael's mother divorced, leaving her to bring up four sons on her own.

As his mother's favourite son, Michael was clean-cut and well behaved. During the hippie era, he wore white shirts and suit jackets. Although raised as a Presbyterian, he graduated a valedictorian for the 1972 Class of Quincy Catholic Boys High School. A brilliant clarinettist, he won a music scholarship to nearby Millikin University College.

After two years, he painted his car army green and joined the Marine Corps. But one stint was all he could stand. Honourably discharged from Camp Lejeune, North Carolina, in 1976, he returned home to study medicine.

At Quincy College, he majored in biology and chemistry, performing push-ups, military style, if criticized by instructors. His senior-year thesis was a meticulous a study of a poisoning case in England. He won the coveted American Chemical Society Award and graduated summa cum laude, wining him a place on the pre-med course at Southern Illinois University.

During his time there, he cut his studies to work for the American Ambulance Service. This gave him privileged access to scenes of death and gore. Car crashes where victims had to be pried from the wreckage particularly excited him.

In 1982, his estranged father died. Michael inherited his father's scrapbook of crashes, coups, sex crimes, arson and riots.

'Hell,' he said. 'I guess Dad wasn't such a bad guy after all.'

He then began a scrapbook of his own. Asked why he engaged in such a blood curdling hobby, he said: 'If I'm ever accused of murder, this will prove I'm mentally unstable.' Meanwhile he was fired by American Ambulance for making a coronary patient walk to the ambulance.

Fabricating reports

Assigned to rotation in the Obstetrics/Gynaecology ward, he often disappeared or showed up late. Under direct supervision of a trained physician, students are graded on their ability to conduct the history and physicals of patients. But it was noticed that he was getting round the patients in double quick time, failing to conduct the simplest of tests and fabricating the reports.

Fearing that he would be flunked, he hired a lawyer and the university agreed to let him graduate, provided he repeat his Obstetrics/Gynaecology rotations. Nevertheless, Swango got an internship at Ohio State University Medical Center, followed by a residency in the department of neurosurgery. There it was noted that he was both incompetent and exhibited a callous attitude towards his patients. One doctor also recorded in his files that the young intern was preoccupied with Nazi history and the genocide of the Jews.

At 10 a.m. on 31 January 1984, Swango turned up unexpectedly at the bedside of neurosurgery patient Ruth Barrick, supposedly to check her IV, asking the nurse to leave. Twenty minutes later, after he had left, the nurse returned to find the patient turning blue, writhing, suffocating. Doctors were able to resuscitate Barrick and she recovered in the Intensive Care Unit, but they were puzzled by her mysterious respiratory failure.

It happened once more a week later, again after Swango had visited her. This time she died. He stood at the foot of the bed while a nurse tried mouth-to-mouth resuscitation.

'That's so disgusting,' he said.

The following day, Swango was seen injecting something into recovering patient Rena Cooper's IV. Moments later, she began shaking violently. Gasping for oxygen, she turned blue. She revived and said that a man answering Swango's description had injected her. Swango denied being there, though a syringe was recovered from a nearby lavatory he had been seen emerging from.

It was noted that there had been a spike in the number of deaths since Swango had been on the ward. These included 19-year-old Cynthia Ann McGee who was found dead in her bed on 14 January

1984, 21-year-old Richard DeLong who succumbed unexpectedly on 21 January and 47-year-old Rein Walker who passed away without warning.

A cursory investigation took place which found that Swango had been the victim of gossip. But he was transferred to another ward where there were more unexplained deaths. On 19 February, 72-year-old Charlotte Warner was found dead in her room after her doctor had told her that she was well enough to be discharged. That same day, Evelyn Pereney began bleeding profusely from body orifices, even through her eyes, after being examined by Michael Swango. The resident physician could find no explanation for the haemorrhaging.

The following day, 22-year-old Anna Mae Popko, who was recovering from a simple intestinal operation, was given a shot by Swango, apparently to increase her blood pressure. The girl's mother did not understand why the doctor had asked her to leave the room. Afterwards, Swango told Mrs Popko: 'She's dead now. You can go look at her.'

After a review, the hospital denied him his residency. He returned to Quincy were he got a job as a paramedic with the Adams County Ambulance Corps. Colleagues were unsettled by his gruesome tales. Then, one morning, Swango brought in an assortment of freshly baked doughnuts and offered them to the other four paramedics on duty. One by one, the entire crew of paramedics were stricken with identical symptoms – stomach cramps, nausea, dizziness, then vomiting – except for Swango who, it was noted, had not partaken.

Two other colleagues were stricken with the same symptoms after Swango had given them a soft drink. In his locker they found ant poison, whose main constituent was arsenic. Setting a trap for him, they prepared a pot of iced tea. After Swango had been left alone with it, they sent the contents to the local coroner. Traces of arsenic were found in it.

The police then searched his apartment and found numerous poisons along with a range of handguns and a number of knives. He was charged with seven counts of aggravated battery. Sentencing him to five years, the judge said: 'It's clearly obvious to me that every man, woman and child in this community or anywhere else that you might go is in jeopardy as long as you are a free person...You deserve the maximum under the law because there is no excuse for what you have done.'

His application for a licence to practise medicine in Illinois was revoked. But while in jail, Swanson agreed to give an interview of the investigative TV programme 20/20.

Barroom brawl

After serving two years, Swango was released for good behaviour. He moved to Newport News, Virginia, where he met 26-year-old divorcee Kristin Kinney, a nurse. After a series of jobs, he was offered a place on a residency programme in Sioux Falls, South Dakota. Asked about his conviction for battery in Illinois, he lied, saying that he had intervened to protect a friend in a barroom brawl.

Swango proposed to Kristin and they moved to Sioux Falls. Things went well, until Swango applied for membership of the American Medical Association. They checked his background and refused it. The reasons were conveyed to Swango's employers. At the same time the 20/20 interview was rebroadcast. He was dismissed.

Kinney then began to suffer headaches and dizziness. These disappeared when she returned to her mother's house in Virginia. Leaving a note, she committed suicide.

Swango moved on to a psychiatric residency programme offered by the State University of New York through its Stony Brook Medical School. Again he explained that his conviction for battery came from a barroom brawl. Within hours of taking up his post, Swango's first patient Dominic Buffalino died mysteriously after recovering from a mild case of pneumonia. Over the next couple of months Aldo Serinei,

Thomas Sammarco and George Siano all died suddenly of heart failure after paralysis struck in the night. Swango had placed a 'Do Not Resuscitate' notice on each of them.

Elsie Harris then found Swango injecting something into her husband Barron's neck. Asked what it was, Swango said: 'Vitamins.' Barron Harris then slipped into a coma from which he never recovered.

When news of the real reasons for Swango's conviction reached Stony Brook, Swango was sacked. He disappeared. The FBI found him working in a water supply facility in Atlanta, Georgia, but before they could obtain a warrant for Swango for falsifying documents to obtain the post at Stony Brook he vanished again.

Swango fled to Zimbabwe where he got a job in a small hospital at Mnene near Bulawayo. He quickly showed his incompetence at the most mundane tasks in healthcare and was sent for a five-month internship at Mpilo Hospital in Bulawayo to brush up on the basics.

When Swango returned to Mnene, he was still sloppy and unpopular. But worse. When Rhoda Mahlamvana entered the hospital with burns from a domestic accident, she was doing well. Then when Swango took over her case, she died. Others, too, died from unexplained heart failure. Swango was suspected.

Patient Keneas Mzezewa awoke one night to find Swango injecting him in the arm. He grew numb. After nurses revived him, he accused Swango of trying to kill him. Swango denied injecting him, though a needle cap was found beside Mzezewa's cot.

Katazo Shava was recovering from a leg operation when Swango came to see him and asked his visitors to leave. They then heard a scream and returned. Shava claimed that Swango had given him something bad in a needle. Swango denied it. Shava died that afternoon of heart failure brought on by paralysis.

Phillimon Chipoko also succumbed to heart failure while having his foot amputated. Virginia Sibanda said she was going into labour when Swango pulled a needle from under his lab coat and injected her. She was wracked with pain, but a healthy child was delivered and she recovered.

When Margaret Zhou died, the nurses insisted the head of the hospital, Dr Christopher Zshiri, go to the police, but Swango hired a lawyer who filed charges of defamation against the hospital. A police search then found lethal drugs in Swango's home.

Swango disappeared. It is thought that he hid out in Zambia, Namibia and Europe. He was then offered a job in Saudi Arabia, but he was arrested by immigration officials changing planes at Chicago's O'Hare Airport on charges of fraud over his application to Stony Brook.

He pled guilty. Imprisoned, the judge ordered that he not be given any duties 'that directly or indirectly require the preparation or delivery of food'.

After interviewing the relatives of the 60 people the FBI suspected Swango had killed, they charged him with killing Thomas Sammarco, Aldo Serinei and George Siano, alleging that he had given them lethal injections that had stopped their hearts. An indictment for the murder of Cynthia McGee followed. The FBI also seized Swango's diary, which showed he killed for pleasure. He loved the 'sweet, husky, close smell of indoor homicide'. He claimed that these murders were 'the only way I have of reminding myself that I'm still alive'.

To avoid the death penalty in the US or Zimbabwe, Swango pleaded guilty to four murders, earning himself four life sentences, three without possibility of parole.

KRISTEN GILBERT

K risten Gilbert was known as a skilled nurse who remained calm in medical emergencies. She won the admiration of those that worked alongside her at the Veterans Administration Medical Center in Northampton, Massachusetts. But in 1990, after she returned from maternity leave, it was noted that the rate of cardiac arrests on Ward C was three times greater than it had been over the previous three years. Patients were dying of cardiac arrest even though they had not suffered from heart complaints previously. So many of them were under the care of Kristen Gilbert that her co-workers began to call her the 'Angel of Death'. At first, it was a joke.

Born Kristen Heather Strickland in Fall River, Massachusetts, in 1967, she showed signs as a teenager of being a pathological liar. For one, she made unfounded claims about being a distant relation of the infamous Lizzie Borden, who reputedly despatched her mother and father with 40 whacks in Fall River in 1892, though she was acquitted.

Former boyfriends accused her of being strange and controlling. They said she even resorted to verbal and physical abuse, or tampering with their cars. When all else failed, she would fake suicide attempts.

Graduating from high school a year and a half early, she enrolled in Bridgewater State College and majored in pre-med, though she later transferred to Greenfield Community College to be closer to her future husband, Glenn Gilbert. While working as a home health aide, she once badly scalded a child with learning difficulties, though no action was taken against her. No one suspected that it might have been deliberate. Then in 1988 she became a registered nurse and eloped with Glenn Gilbert. Their marriage was full of rows, however, and on one occasion she chased him around the house with a butcher's knife.

Soon after their marriage, Kristen got a job at the Veterans Administration Medical Center in Northampton, Massachusetts, working on Ward C. Well liked, she remembered birthdays and organized gift exchanges during the holidays. She distinguished herself early on and was featured in the magazine VA *Practitioner* in April 1990.

Deaths start to climb

Everything changed after the birth of her first child, when she was switched to the 4 p.m. to midnight shift. Deaths during her shifts then began to climb, though she still showed skill and confidence during these emergencies. However, one doctor refused to let her treat any more of his patients.

After the birth of her second son in 1993, the Gilberts' marriage ran into difficulties. She had taken a fancy to James Perrault, a security guard at the hospital.

Under VA rules, security had to be on hand during any medical emergency, so when there was a cardiac arrest on Ward C he would be called, giving her the chance to impress him with her medical skills and flirt with him. They would also have drinks together after her shift ended.

When they became lovers, it was alleged that an AIDS patient suddenly died of a heart attack so that she could leave early to go on a date with Perrault. Gilbert's husband Glenn then found his food tasted odd and was convinced that she was trying to kill him. Soon afterwards, Kristen moved out of the marital home to be closer to Perrault and she then filed for divorce.

The high mortality rate on Ward C put all the nurses under suspicion. While the authorities were searching for some explanation, it was noted that stocks of the drug epinephrine – a synthetic form of adrenaline – were going missing. It was a heart stimulant that could cause cardiac arrest if injected unnecessarily. Three fellow nurses then reported their suspicions to the authorities.

Hoax bomb calls

While the matter was under investigation, Gilbert bought a device to disguise her voice and then called the hospital to say that bombs had been planted there. Staff and patients, many of whom were sick and elderly, had to be evacuated. No explosives were found, but the hoax calls always occurred on Perrault's shift.

It was not long before the police linked Gilbert to the calls. Perrault was then summoned before a grand jury, where he testified against his lover. At that point, Glenn Gilbert asked investigators to come to his house and search Kristen's former pantry, where they found the *Handbook of Poisoning*. Meanwhile, Gilbert was temporarily placed in a psychiatric ward at Arbour Hospital for the third time in a month.

She later turned up at Glenn Gilbert's house and threatened him with her car keys. A court order then confined her to Bayside Medical Center. When she was released, she was arrested on a charge of making bomb threats. She was then sentenced to 15 months at Danbury Federal Prison and treated for psychiatric problems.

Patients' bodies exhumed

While she was in prison, investigators began to exhume some of the bodies of those who had died on her shift. They were found to contain epinephrine, though the deceased patients had no history of heart complaints.

Gilbert seemed to be an exemplary employee, but when she changed shifts, the death rate went up.

In November 1998, aged 30, she was indicted for the murders of four men and the attempted murders of three others. However, the United States attorney said that 37 men had died during her shifts between January 1995 and February 1996. Her potential body count was much greater. In the seven years she had worked at the VA hospital, 350 patients had died on her shifts and she was thought to have been responsible for 80 of the deaths.

In all, the prosecution brought 70 witnesses and 200 pieces of evidence against her.

The witnesses included her ex-husband, who said she had confessed to the murders.

Perrault also testified against her, saying that she had told him during a telephone conversation: 'I did it. You wanted to know, I killed all those guys by injection.'

The defence maintained that she had only said that after suffering psychiatric problems following the break-up of their tempestuous affair. There were no witnesses to Gilbert administering the drug, so all the evidence was circumstantial.

'The four murders were especially cruel and heinous,' said US Attorney David Stern, citing the case of 41-year-old Kenneth Cutting, who was blind and had multiple sclerosis. Gilbert had asked a supervisor if she could leave work early if he were to die. He died 40 minutes later and empty ampoules of epinephrine were found nearby. Prosecutors maintained that Gilbert was also on duty when 37 of the 63 patients on Ward C died and that she tried to cover her tracks by falsifying medical records.

Explaining why Gilbert was standing trial in just seven cases, Assistant US Attorney Ariane Vuono told jurors: 'These seven victims were veterans. They were vulnerable. They were the perfect victims. When Kristen Gilbert killed them, she used the perfect poison.'

Lawyers for Gilbert argued that the patients died of natural causes. They said Gilbert had been falsely accused by her co-workers, who were upset that she was having an extramarital affair.

'She was scorned by her peers and her co-workers,' defence attorney David Hoose told the jury. 'You must understand how rumours about what was going on in Kristen Gilbert's life affected, coloured and tainted everyone's opinions of what was going on in Ward C.'

Life imprisonment

Despite her lawyers' pleas, in March 2001 Kristen Gilbert was found guilty of three counts of first-degree murder, one count of second-degree murder and two counts of attempted murder. While there was no death penalty in the state of Massachusetts, the crimes had taken place on federal property, so she faced the prospect of execution – ironically, by lethal injection. Assistant US Attorney William Welch called Gilbert a 'shell of a human being' who deserved to die for the cold and calculating way she murdered her victims.

The defence argued that she did not need to die, because it would be punishment enough to lead a life 'where you can't walk out into a field, or see snow or play with a puppy'. Her father and grandmothers also pleaded for her life, saying a death sentence would be devastating to them and Gilbert's two sons.

'It is easier to incite good and decent people to kill when their target is not human but a demon,' said defence attorney Paul Weinberg. 'Kristen Gilbert is not a monster, she is a human being.'

This won little sympathy from the relatives of the victims.

Claire Jagadowski, widow of 66-year-old Stanley Jagadowski, told the judge: 'I still listen for his key in the door. Now I have to face old age alone.'

Gilbert herself declined to take the stand and wept softly when the decision was handed down.

After six hours' deliberation, the jury decided against the death penalty, though the decision was not unanimous. Instead, the judge sentenced her to four consecutive terms of life imprisonment without possibility of parole, plus 20 years. There was no audible reaction in the courtroom. Her parents wept and the victims' families sat stone-faced.

'It's a very bittersweet day when you think your daughter is going to get life imprisonment instead of the death penalty,' said Gilbert's father, Richard Strickland.

Gilbert dropped her appeal after the US Supreme Court ruled that she risked the death penalty on retrial. Her life sentence would be served at the Carswell Federal Medical Center in Fort Worth, Texas.

KATHLEEN FOLBIGG

Kathleen Megan Folbigg has the doubtful distinction of being Australia's first convicted female serial killer. She is imprisoned at Silverwater Woman's Correctional Centre, 14 km (9 miles) from downtown Sydney.

Born in Sydney on 14 June 1967, Kathleen was placed in a church orphanage before her second birthday. At the age of three, she was adopted by the Marlboroughs, a loving foster family in suburban Newcastle. Kathleen – or Kathy, as she preferred to be called – was not the best student. She left school before her sixteenth birthday in order to take the first in a series of low-wage, low-skilled jobs. Within six years, she had met and married her husband, Craig Folbigg, a steel worker. The newly-weds set up home in the Newcastle suburb of Mayfield.

Kathy was pregnant by the time the couple's first anniversary came along. She gave birth to a baby boy named Caleb on the first day of February 1989. The young mother had experienced a good full term pregnancy, which had resulted in the birth of a seemingly healthy child. Yet four days after Caleb was born the new mother and her child were back at the hospital. Kathy told doctors that while she had been feeding the newborn baby she had noticed that he had been having some trouble breathing. Caleb was diagnosed as having a 'lazy larynx', which was not seen as a serious condition.

Tragedy strikes

Fourteen days passed without incident. Then shortly before 3 a.m. on 19 February Craig was awoken by Kathy's screams. They were coming from the baby's room. His wife was standing at the side of the crib. She was weeping over Caleb's lifeless body. The cause of death, after just 18 days of life, was listed as SIDS – Sudden Infant Death Syndrome.

By September, seven months after Caleb's death, Kathy was again pregnant. On 3 June 1990, she gave birth to Patrick, another baby boy. At that stage, there was nothing to suggest that Patrick was not completely healthy. However, shortly after 3 a.m. on 19 October 1990, Craig was again jolted out of slumber by his wife's screams. Running to the baby's room, he saw Kathy standing over the cot. Patrick was not breathing. The steel worker picked the baby up and began resuscitation. Though the baby survived, no one was able to determine the cause of the medical emergency. During the myriad tests that followed, the baby was discovered to be epileptic and blind. Clearly, Patrick had not been as healthy as the doctors had originally believed.

On 13 February 1991, just days before the second anniversary of Caleb's death, Craig was at work when he received a frantic phone call from Kathy. 'It's happened again,' she said. He reached home just as the ambulance arrived. This time the father could do nothing to save his son. At eight months of age, Patrick was dead. After an autopsy had been conducted, the cause of the child's death was recorded as an epileptic fit, which had resulted in an 'acute asphyxiating event'.

Following this sad affair the couple moved to Thornton, a suburb of Maitland, which lay approximately 159 km (99 miles) to the north of Sydney. It was there, on 14 October 1992, that the third Folbigg child was born. This time, Kathy gave birth to a baby girl, who was named

Sarah Kathleen. But disaster struck again. In the early hours of 30 August 1993, the ten-month-old infant stopped breathing. According to Kathy, baby Sarah had caught some sort of cold and was having trouble sleeping.

After losing their daughter, the Folbiggs moved yet again. This time they settled in Singleton, a town on the Hunter River, about an hour's drive from Newcastle. In the space of only four and a half years the couple had endured the deaths of three children. It was two years before Kathy became pregnant again. Then on 7 August 1997 she gave birth to Laura, another baby girl. At first Laura appeared to be quite healthy, just like the Folbigg children that had come before her. In view of the past tragedies, however, her sleep patterns and her breathing were monitored very closely throughout August and into September. Unlike her dead siblings, Laura managed to celebrate her first birthday. In fact, she lived nearly 19 months before developing what her mother described as a cold. Then at about noon on 1 March 1999, Kathy called for an ambulance. The attendants arrived to find the mother 'performing CPR on her daughter on the breakfast bar'. It was all in vain – Laura was dead. This time, however, Laura's death could not be written off to SIDS: she was simply too old. After performing an autopsy, the coroner ordered a police investigation.

Meanwhile, the strain on the Folbigg marriage had taken its toll. Kathy left her husband, taking very few possessions with her. Much of what she left behind was personal in nature, nothing more so than the diaries that Craig found while he was cleaning the house. Reading their contents, the abandoned husband said that he wanted to vomit. The diaries contained the thoughts of a tormented woman, who had often been jealous of the attention her babies were receiving. Kathy recorded 'flashes of rage, resentment and hatred' towards her children. Concerning Laura, she wrote:

> I feel like the worst mother on this earth. Scared that she will
> leave me now. Like Sarah did. I knew I was short-tempered

Kathy Folbigg admitted to having 'flashes of rage, resentment and hatred' towards her children.

and cruel sometimes to her and she left. With a bit of help. She's a fairly good-natured baby – thank goodness, it has saved her from the fate of her siblings. I'm sure she's met everyone and they've told her, don't be a bad or sickly kid, mum may, you know, crack. They've warned her – good.

Kathy's diaries were handed over to Bernard Ryan, the detective assigned to the case. They would ultimately be used as evidence against her in a court of law.

It took two years to put the case together. Tests determined that none of the four Folbigg children had suffered any genetic or viral disorders. Further investigation revealed that all of the deaths were inconsistent with SIDS – each child had been lying face upwards and all of them had been still warm when the ambulance attendants had arrived. During the course of the investigation, Ryan uncovered a very disturbing story from Kathy's past. In December 1968, a couple of weeks before Christmas, Kathy's father had killed her mother. She was stabbed 24 times outside her home in suburban Sydney. After his murderous act, Kathy's father reportedly knelt down beside the body. He kissed his dead lover and whispered, 'I'm sorry, darling. I had to do it.' According to a witness he then said, 'I had to kill her because she'd kill my child.' The child in question was Kathy.

It is not so surprising that Kathy knew nothing of the tragedy until her late teens. Her birth parents were poles apart from the caring couple that had adopted her. Kathy's birth father was a petty thief with ties to organized crime, while her birth mother was addicted to gambling and alcohol. The uncovering of the tragedy that had taken place between Kathy's parents made one particular passage in the diary stand out: 'Obviously, I am my father's daughter.'

Justice served

On 19 April 2001 Kathy was arrested and charged with the murders of all four of her children. When her foster mother learned of the arrest, she sent Kathy all of her childhood photographs, accompanied by a letter. 'Kathleen Megan, I WILL NEVER FORGIVE YOU,' she wrote. The prosecution presented the medical evidence that had been amassed over the previous two years, adding that the diaries were a 'partial admission of guilt'. Witnesses, including Kathy's foster sister, Lea Brown, supported the self-portrait that Kathy had penned. It was noted, for example, that Kathy had expressed no real grief at the funerals of her four children. The court was also presented with a video tape that showed a seemingly healthy Laura swimming in her pool on the afternoon before her death.

In spite of all of the evidence to the contrary, the defence argued that all four Folbigg children had been sickly. They called a forensic pathologist named Roger Byard as a witness, but even he was forced to admit that it was possible that each of the children had died from deliberate suffocation. On 21 May 2003, Kathleen Folbigg was found guilty on three counts of murder, one count of manslaughter and one count of maliciously inflicting grievous bodily harm. She was sentenced to 40 years imprisonment, with the possibility of parole after 30 years. On appeal, her sentence was reduced to a prison sentence of 30 years, with a non-parole period of 25 years.

Craig Folbigg obtained a divorce and has since remarried. He was offered more than $200,000 for his story, but he turned it down, explaining that he just wanted to get on with his life.

CHARLES CULLEN

The usual cliché about serial killers is how normal they always seemed before their ghastly secrets were uncovered. Not so Charles Cullen. Few people could have appeared more out of step with their surroundings. Cullen worked for 16 years at hospitals in New Jersey and Pennsylvania, during which time he admitted to killing as many as 40 patients, but that could be just the tip of the iceberg.

Police suspect he could have given drug overdoses to as many as 400 elderly patients, which would make him the worst serial killer ever in North America, but due to lack of evidence this figure may never be confirmed.

Danger Signs

Charles Cullen was a shy and unhappy child. The youngest of eight children, he was born in West Orange, New Jersey, on 22 February 1960. His father, a bus driver, died when he was only seven months old and two of his siblings passed away while he was still young.

The danger signs were there from an early age. When he was nine, Cullen tried to take his own life by swallowing the contents of a chemistry set. Later he told police he had tried to commit suicide on at least 20 separate occasions (though it would only have taken one attempt had he shown the same shabby expertise he used to despatch his mainly aged victims).

In 5th grade, he revealed the depth of his adolescent angst with an unpublished book called *Infinity Years Will Never Know* about growing up in a world devoid of meaning, and he began compulsively reading and re-reading Dostoevsky's *Crime and Punishment* which details the mental torment of a student who commits murder.

At the age of 17, he suffered a crushing blow when his mother was killed in a car crash. Cullen's behaviour became increasingly off-kilter. Bullied at school, he went to a party where he laced his tormentors' drinks with rat poison. It was a practice run for what was to follow.

Dropping out of high school, Cullen joined the US Navy in April 1978, enlisting as a ballistic missiles technician. He came through the stringent psychological test for submariners with flying colours and was assigned to a Poseidon missiles unit on board the nuclear submarine U.S.S. *Woodrow Wilson*. Here he was christened with the nickname 'Fish-belly white' due to the deathly pallor of his complexion. His bunkmate, Marlin Emswiler, acknowledged Cullen had no friends. 'Charlie hung out with Charlie. Kept saying he wanted to become a nurse because he liked helping people.'

One day, Cullen was discovered by crew members at the missile control panel of the nuclear submarine, wearing a green surgical gown, surgical mask and latex gloves pilfered from the ship's medical cabinet. He was transferred to the U.S.S. *Canopus*, and discharged from the Navy in March 1984 after yet another suicide attempt.

One-word answers

He was now free to follow his morbid medical bent. He gained a degree from the Mountainside School of Nursing, Montclair, NJ which he left in 1987, the same year he began his first nursing job at the St Barnabus Medical Center, Livingston, NJ.

A colleague recalled his inability to deal with normal social situations. 'You'd ask him, "Are you married" or something like that, and get one-word answers.' In 1988 he killed for the first time. His victim was 72-year-old judge John Yengo, who was injected with a drug called Lidocaine. The death was recorded in newspapers of the time as being 'a case of Stevens-Johnson syndrome', a rare allergic reaction. In 1992, Cullen was fired, probably for randomly contaminating bags of intravenous fluid with insulin. No one seems to be quite sure.

Due to the shortage of nurses and the fact that, for legal reasons, honest work appraisals were seldom passed on between medical companies, Cullen never had trouble finding work. Over the next 11 years, he had nine separate jobs. Like many 'angels of mercy', he discovered a taste for working 'graveyard shifts' on cardiac and intensive-care wards where he was left without supervision and where people died all the time. The atmosphere of trust in hospitals allowed him plenty of leeway.

In 1993 his estranged wife Adrienne filed for a restraining order against him: she claimed he had spiked drinks with lighter fluid, left his daughters at a babysitter's for a week and shown cruelty towards their two Yorkshire terriers, zipping one up in a bowling bag. His debts mounted steadily as he took to drink and his life fell apart.

Bizarre behaviour

Psychologists say Cullen killed to relieve stress and this does seem to be borne out by the facts. Accused of domestic violence, he murdered three elderly women by giving them overdoses of the heart medication digoxin. Faced with a lie detector test to show he had not neglected his children or abused alcohol in their presence, he killed 85-year-old Mary Natoli.

After a social worker recommended all visits to his children be supervised, he killed Helen Dean, 91, who was recovering from surgery for colon cancer. Her son Larry recalled a thin male nurse entering the room and telling him to leave. When Larry returned, his mother said, 'He stuck me,' and showed him an injection mark on her thigh. Next day she grew ill and died.

Cullen's behaviour grew more bizarre. Neighbours talked about him chasing cats down the street at dead of night, muttering to himself and making faces. He harassed and stalked a fellow nurse when she turned down his offer of an engagement ring after just one date.

Charles Cullen.

In every hospital where he worked Cullen aroused suspicions. He was fired from one for stealing vials of medicine. At St Luke's Hospital, Bethlehem, Pennsylvania, a group of nurses reported their suspicions that Cullen has been using drugs to kill patients. The case was dropped.

At Somerset Medical Center, NJ, computer records showed Cullen was accessing the records of patients he was not assigned to as well as requesting medications that patients had not been prescribed. When Jin Kyung Han, a 40-year-old cancer patient, went into cardiac arrest, doctors were surprised to find high levels of digoxin in her system despite the fact they had taken her off the drug.

Cullen was fired from Somerset on 31 October 2003 for falsifying his job application, but he remained under surveillance. On 12 December he was arrested and charged with the murder of Father Florian Gall, a 68-year-old Roman Catholic priest who died from a digoxin overdose, as well as the attempted murder of Han. The floodgates opened and Cullen confessed to a catalogue of murders, but not to all of them. He had blocked most of the fatalities from memory... or so he said.

On 2 March 2006 Cullen was sentenced to 11 consecutive life sentences for the murder of 22 and the attempted murder of three persons in New Jersey; this will make him eligible for parole after 397 years in jail.

KIMBERLY CLARK SAENZ

In April 2008, inspectors of the Texas Department of Health Services were alerted to problems at the DaVita Dialysis clinic in Lufkin, Texas. A member of the emergency services sent an anonymous letter saying: 'In the last two weeks, we have transported 16 patients. This seems a little abnormal and disturbing to my med crews. Could these calls be investigated by you?'

Reviewing the clinic's record, it was found that there had only been two emergency calls in the previous 15 months, but they had been called out 30 times that month – seven for cardiac problems. Four people had already died. On 1 April, Clara Strange and Thelma Metcalf died after suffering cardiac arrest. On the 16th, Garlin Kelley suffered cardiac arrest and died two days later at the hospital, while Graciela Castañeda lost consciousness during treatment.

On 22 April, Cora Bryant suffered cardiac arrest and died three months later at the hospital. The following day, Marie Bradley suffered a severe drop in blood pressure. Then on 26 April, Opal Few died after suffering cardiac arrest and Debra Oates experienced multiple symptoms and a severe drop in blood pressure.

Concerned about the mortality rate, DaVita sent in a new supervisor from Houston named Amy Clinton who promptly took charge. When

34-year-old Kimberly Saenz arrived on shift at 4.30 a.m. on 28 April, she was distressed to find that she had effectively been demoted. She was in tears. Previously, she had the run of the place. Her job as a nurse was to move from patient to patient, injecting medication into the dialysis lines and ports with a syringe. Now she was to clean up after patients, wiping up blood and vomit.

At around 6 a.m., Marva Rhone and Carolyn Risinger came into the clinic. Like other patients with failed kidneys, they spent hours on the dialysis machine cleansing their blood three times a week. It was a matter of life and death.

Two other patients, Lurlene Hamilton and Linda Hall, sitting nearby, noticed that Saenz was nervous. They saw her squat down and pour bleach into her cleaning bucket. Then they saw her draw up the caustic liquid into a syringe. At the very least, they thought this insanitary. But then they said they saw her inject the contents of the syringe into the dialysis lines of Rhone and Risinger.

Hamilton told Amy Clinton what she and seen, adding: 'I'm a little nervous right now, and I'm worried because she's assigned to me.'

Linda Hall also reported that Saenz had filled a syringe and injected Rhone's 'saline' line. Both witnesses said they saw Saenz dispose of the syringes in the DaVita sharps containers. Shortly after, Rhone and Risinger experienced a dramatic drop in blood pressure.

After speaking to Hamilton and Hall, Clinton asked Saenz whether she had administered any medication that day. Saenz said no. When asked about the bleach, Saenz explained that she 'was drawing up bleach to mix for her containers' that she had on the floor. Three syringes collected from the sharp container tested positive for bleach. She then acknowledged using a syringe to extract the bleach from its container because she was concerned about being precise and following procedures. A solution of bleach was commonly used to sterilize equipment in the clinic, but she adamantly denied ever injecting bleach into a patient.

Kimberly Saenz was seen injecting bleach into the dialysis lines of patients in the hospital where she worked.

Saenz was sent home. The following day the clinic was closed as an investigation was carried out. A meeting was called to inform the employees. All of them turned up except for Saenz. Co-worker Werlan Guillory phoned her and asked: 'Where are you? Are you coming to the meeting?'

Saenz said she could not make it.

'I'm a chaperone at my daughter's field day,' she said.

Guillory expressed concern that Saenz might lose her job, but Saenz simply responded: 'Okay.'

After the meeting, Guillory went to find Saenz. He said she was uncharacteristically unkempt and acted as if she did not recognize him. She was crying and told him she 'didn't kill those people'. This was unexpected as, at that point, no one had made any allegations that someone was killing patients. Guillory described Saenz as seeming 'like she had lost all the hope in the world'.

A chequered past

Saenz had held her entry-level position as a Licensed Vocational Nurse (LVN) at the clinic for nine months by then. Previously, she had been fired from another hospital in Lufkin for stealing the opioid Demerol, which was found in her handbag. She had also been arrested for public intoxication and criminal trespass, and the police had been called for domestic disturbances involving her husband, Mark Kevin Saenz. He filed for divorce and had obtained a restraining order against Saenz in June 2007, just a few months before she began at DaVita. An examination of the records revealed that 84 per cent of the time patients had suffered from chest pain or cardiac arrest, Saenz had been on duty.

Questioned by Lufkin police officers, Saenz was noticeably upset that two patients had accused her of giving them another patient's medication. Asked why she had not attended the meeting, Saenz said she was scared to go to work because DaVita 'can't tell us what's going on, and I'm doing everything by the book, and I'm scared because I have a licence'. She added: 'If I'm doing something wrong, I want to know that I'm doing something wrong 'cause I don't want to kill somebody.'

When asked whether she had administered any medications during her shift on 28 April, Saenz said: 'I did give [Rhone] some saline, only because she said she was cramping.'

She said she opened her saline line because her nurse wasn't there. This was recorded on the patient's chart, but the patient's blood pressure didn't really go down that much, and then she said she felt nauseous.

The officers asked Saenz if she had any theories about the underlying cause of the injuries. She mentioned a 'bleach loop' and wondered whether 'our machines are hooked up and they have some bleach in them.'

She went on to explain the clinic's 'bleaching procedures' – a medicine cup was used to pour bleach into a container where it was diluted. Sponges were then soaked in the liquid and used to wipe the chairs. Although Saenz understood the policy was to use a medicine cup to measure the bleach, when pushed by the officer on whether she had ever used a syringe, Saenz acknowledged doing so.

'Sometimes I do when I can't find the little medicine cups,' she said. 'There wasn't any cups up there that day. But if you use a syringe, 10 cc, then you're going to have to, you know, put it in the receptacle. So I took my bleach and I just poured it and then I pulled up to 10 cc, 'cause I knew that would be like 10 ml.'

Other than Saenz's own statement, there was no evidence that the supply of measuring cups was depleted. Saenz further explained the monitors at the facility made her nervous, and she wanted to ensure that she was precisely following procedures.

Tests by the US Food and Drug Administration showed the presence of bleach in the dialysis lines, and the victims tested positive for bleach also. Saenz was indicted on five counts of murder and five counts of aggravated assault for the injuries to other patients. The deadly weapon Saenz used, the indictment said, was sodium hypochlorite – bleach. Even while she was out on bail, Saenz had applied for other healthcare jobs in violation of her bail conditions.

She swore an affidavit that she had no previous felony record. But documents filed by Angelina County District Attorney Clyde Herrington listed about a dozen instances of wrongdoing. They included allegations Saenz overused prescription drugs, had substance abuse and addiction problems, was fired at least four times from healthcare jobs and put false information on an employment application.

Investigators found internet searches on Saenz's computer about bleach poisoning in blood and whether bleach could be detected in dialysis lines. Saenz told the grand jury she had been concerned about the patients' deaths and looked up bleach poisoning references to see 'if this was happening, what would be the side effects'.

Saenz did not take the stand in her own defence at the trial. But a recording of the testimony she gave before a grand jury was played, where she said she felt 'railroaded' by the clinic and 'would never inject bleach into a patient'.

The defence insisted that Saenz had no motive to kill.

'Kimberly Saenz is a good nurse, a compassionate, a caring individual who assisted her patients and was well liked,' said defence attorney T. Ryan Deaton. He argued that Saenz was being targeted by the clinic's owner for faulty procedures at the facility, including improper water purification, and suggested that officials at the clinic fabricated evidence against her.

Trouble in the workplace

Before the trial, Deaton fought for the jury to have access to a US Department of Health and Human Services report from May 2008 that was heavily critical of DaVita's practices. But the report was ruled inadmissible by District Judge Barry Bryan.

According to the report, from 1 December 2007 to 28 April 2008, when Saenz had been there, the facility had 19 deaths compared to 25 for the whole of 2007. Those numbers put the facility at a mortality rate of seven per cent, which was above the state average.

The clinic was also not keeping proper records of adverse occurrences, the report stated. From 1 September 2007 to 26 April 2008, there was a total of 102 DaVita patients transported by ambulance to local hospitals during or immediately following dialysis. Of those, 60 did not have a complete adverse occurrence report.

The report went on to say that, based on record reviews and nursing staff interviews, the clinic 'did not demonstrate competence in monitoring patients during treatment alerting nurses or physicians of changes to a patient's condition and following the physician's orders for the dialysis treatment'.

However, the prosecution described claims that Saenz was being set up by her employer as 'absolutely ridiculous'. They described her as a depressed and disgruntled employee who complained about specific patients, including some of those who died or were injured.

Clinic employees reported Saenz was not happy with her employment at DaVita. Several people reported Saenz was frustrated when DaVita had reassigned her to the lesser position of patient care technician. Saenz herself considered administration of medications much less stressful and felt she was being treated unfairly by DaVita. During her shift on 28 April, Saenz was described as 'teary-eyed' in reaction to her lesser assignment.

In addition to Saenz's displeasure with her demotion, she expressed her aversion to some of the DaVita patients. One employee testified Saenz specifically voiced her dislike of Strange, Metcalf, Kelley, Few, Oates, Rhone and Risinger, all of whom either died or were injured during treatment that April. The records substantiated that during each of the alleged incidents, Saenz was at the DaVita facility functioning either as a patient care technician or as a nurse responsible for preparing medications for each patient.

Taken off the streets – forever

The prosecution also maintained that there were more victims, but detectives could only obtain medical waste from two weeks prior to 28 April 2008, so there was inadequate evidence to raise further indictments against Saenz. Nevertheless, an epidemiologist from the Centers for Disease Control and Prevention statistically connected Saenz to other adverse health events to patients.

'The only days there were deaths in April, she was there,' said prosecutor Clyde Herrington. 'Dialysis patients are sick, but every source of information we can find says it is very unusual for patients to die during dialysis treatment.'

He pointed out that the state did not have to prove motive to get a conviction. However, the prosecution had talked to a registered nurse who studied more than 100 healthcare killers. The most common method they used was injecting a patient with some type of medication or substance.

'Criminal behaviour is something we've been trying to understand since Cain killed Abel,' Herrington said. 'Only when the healthcare killer confesses do we know motive.'

Speculating, Herrington said he believed that Saenz was a troubled woman with marital problems who lashed out because of job dissatisfaction.

'From talking to some of the folks who worked with her, it sounded like her husband didn't want her to quit [the clinic],' Herrington said. 'She was depressed. She was frustrated, and I think she took those frustrations out on the patients.'

On 30 March 2012, Kimberly Saenz was convicted of killing five patients and deliberately injuring three others. She faced the death penalty. Addressing the jury, another of Saenz's attorneys, Steve Taylor, asked for leniency, saying: 'She's never getting out no matter what you do.'

He reminded jurors Saenz had been free on bail during the trial and prosecutors had failed to show she would present a future danger – one of the questions jurors are required to answer when deciding a death penalty.

'Society is protected,' said Taylor. 'You will never see her again.'

The prosecution made no real effort to urge the jurors to impose the death penalty.

'I know you'll reach a verdict that's just and in accordance with the law,' said Herrington after showing the jury photographs of some of the victims on a large screen in the courtroom. Ultimately, they chose to impose a life sentence for each of the murders, plus 21 years' imprisonment for each of the aggravated assaults. The Court of Appeals of Texas in San Antonio confirmed the trial court's verdict.

VICTORINO CHUA

In early July 2011, the police began investigating the deaths of
three patients at Stepping Hill Hospital in Stockport, Greater
Manchester, after saline solution was found to have been tampered
with. Insulin had been added. This would reduce the level of glucose
in the bloodstream often to fatal effect.

After contaminated saline solution was administered 84-year-old
George Keep, 71-year-old Arnold Lancaster and 44-year-old Tracey
Arden all died, though each had underlying medical conditions. Later
that month, two more patients died in the same way, bringing the
death count to five. Sixteen others were found to have been affected
by the contamination.

Armed guards were stationed at the hospital while Greater
Manchester Police brought in 60 detectives to investigate. The staff
were forced to work in pairs while administering medication and
CCTV was installed.

On 20 July, 27-year-old nurse Rebecca Leighton was arrested and
charged with three counts of criminal damage with intent to endanger
life. She remained in custody for six weeks until, on 2 September, the
charges were dropped. However, after admitting stealing medication
from the hospital she was sacked.

After she had been dismissed, another suspicious death occurred on 31 December. Eighty-two-year-old Bill Dickson had died on New Year's Eve and 46-year-old Victorino Chua was arrested for altering medical forms and giving a patient extra medication. The patient who was given additional amounts of medication was monitored by hospital staff and had since been discharged. By then 650 people had been interview in connection to the enquiry.

Chua was charged under section 23 of the Offences Against the Person Act – namely unlawfully or maliciously administering or causing to be taken by another person any poison or destructive or noxious thing so as to endanger life or inflict grievous bodily harm. By then it was suspected that 22 patients on the acute care wards for seriously ill patients had been poisoned and seven had died as a result.

Bitter nurse confession

After applying for extra time to interrogate Filipino-born father-of-two Chua, the police released him on bail. Colleagues said Chua, who was known as Vic, was very caring towards patients. But in his kitchen drawer, the police found a rambling 13-page letter in pidgin English that he said he had written on the advice of a counsellor to release tension. Chua called it a 'bitter nurse confession'.

Chua was born in the Philippines on 30 October 1965, the third of six children. He felt neglected. His father contracted three other marriages and had other children, while the young Victorino did not get on with his mother Vanetta. While his father, the manager of a computer business, was a good breadwinner, Victorino's parents left their kids to fend for themselves like animals.

At high school, he got into drink and drugs, but his grandmother pushed him towards the medical profession. He did not want to be a nurse, but she said if he got his nursing certificate she would pay for him to go on to train as a doctor.

When Victorino was 21, his father died of a heart attack. This was a wake-up call for Chua and he signed up for a nursing course at Manila's prestigious Metropolitan Medical Center. Wealthy people from less well developed countries came for treatment there. Even patients from the US came as it was cheaper than hospitals in the States.

The hours were long. Chua rose at 4 a.m. to give his grandmother a bath before heading off for his studies, never returning home before 7 p.m. Nevertheless, he made friends with doctors and persuaded them to give free health care to members of his family. He spent his spare time running errands for wealthy students, scoring drugs for his classmates and spending the profits on designer clothes.

After a year, he passed his exams to become a nurse, though it is suspected that he paid another student to sit the examinations for him. Nevertheless in 1989 he had a BSc in nursing from Galong Medical Center College of Nursing and, at age 24, he was a registered nurse.

He worked in various medical centres around Manila. To supplement his wages, he sold stolen healthcare produces, electronic goods and designer clothes, billing himself as a Robin Hood figure, stealing from the rich and giving to the poor. He kept a diary of his escapes and seems to have been a hit with the girls.

In 1996, he married Marianne in a civil union. They had two daughters. But he got caught stealing and was fired from his nursing job. For a time, he made a living as a car salesman but, eager to return to nursing, he took a job in a nursing home in Warrington, Cheshire in northwest England. However, by this time he had developed a drug addiction and started stealing painkillers.

He moved on in 2005 possibly after being caught stealing drugs, but he got good references. Three years later he was working as a nurse in Stockport. There he got into an altercation with a colleague and appeared at a disciplinary hearing. He lied to save his neck, but he soon left the job under a cloud.

Addiction to drugs

On 1 June 2009, Chua started at Stepping Hill Hospital, where a staff of over 5,700 treated some half-a-million patients a year. About a year into the job he went into counselling for depression, possibly brought on by his addiction to drugs. He took sleeping pills and painkillers for knee and back pain. The counselling did little to help. On top of that, he relationship with his wife and daughters became strained.

On 7 July 2011, 44-year-old mother-of-two Tracy Arden was admitted to Stepping Hill Hospital with a mild chest infection. Although she had been battling with multiple sclerosis since the age of 32, the staff assumed she would recover and leave the hospital in no time. But they administered a saline drip which, in the privacy of her room, Chua contaminated with insulin. This induced hypoglycemic or insulin shock. With her brain deprived of the glucose it needed, she slipped into a coma and died within the hour. Though her sudden death was unexpected, no one suspected Chua.

Later that month Chua added insulin to the saline drip of 83-year-old Alfred Weaver. He died of hypoglycaemic shock ten days later. He did the same to four other males.

Then he broadened his range of victims. Instead of killing just his own patients, he injected insulin into the sealed drug vials known as ampoules so that other nurses would unknowingly administer spiked drugs to their patients.

Aged 86, Daphne Harlowe was admitted to Stepping Hill Hospital after suffering a fall. Within a day of her admission, she experienced a severe hypoglycemic attack. Twenty-four-year-old Zubia Aslam suffered a similar attack. It was found that Zubia's ampoule had a large amount of insulin in it. Meanwhile Chua went on to inject insulin into saline bags so his colleagues would do more of his dirty work for him.

By 12 July, Stepping Hill Hospital was in uproar over the number of patients slipping into hypoglycaemic comas. A nurse discovered several saline bags that were leaking – clear evidence they had been contaminated. Hospital staff then tested the ampoules and found insulin in them. They called the police and an investigation was launched. As part of it, a forensic scientist found that small V-shaped holes had been cut into the rubber resealable connector typically found at the bottom edge of saline bags.

Also two puncture holes were found in the inner membrane of the bag, which appeared to be made by a hypodermic needle. Further testing showed that a glucose bag, saline bag and an antibiotic bag also had puncture holes, while another saline bag had been contaminated with a local anaesthetic called Lidocaine.

After beefing up the security, investigators examined the medical records and blood samples associated with all cases of hypoglycemia at the hospital. They cross-referenced the dates of the attacks with the work records thousands of hospital staff. On 20 July 2011, the police felt confident enough to make an arrest. Unfortunately, they got the wrong person.

Forensic evidence showed that Rebecca Leighton had handle some of the contaminated IV products. The press quickly dubbed her the Angel of Death. It took six weeks before she was cleared of the murders. Although she was fired, she sued Greater Manchester Police for leaking her name to the media.

Five months after Leighton was released, Chua struck again. At the beginning of January 2012, he was working the night shift at the A3 ward of the hospital when he got into an argument with an elderly patient's daughter. When she insisted that Chua procure a heart monitor for her mother, he threw it angrily on a table.

The following morning, staff discovered that the patient's prescription charts had been altered. Taking a closer look, nurses noticed that the charts of five other female patients, aged 79 to 92, had also been tampered with. Alterations had been made to the prescribed dosages of drugs. These were doubled or even tripled. In one case a new drug was added which could have caused a heart attack. Thankfully, the intended victim survived with no significant harm.

While Chua continued to endanger patients of Stepping Hill Hospital, police were still investigating the original poisonings. By then, over a hundred detectives were working on the case. Due to the random nature of the murders, they cast the net wide. During the autumn of 2011, 1,177 people were interviewed. Police took 3,291 statements. And 5,394 items were collected as exhibits at the trial. The prosecution file grew to over 30,000 pages.

Investigators eliminated suspects one by one until only Chua was left. They sent a team to the Philippines which turned up his criminal past.

On 5 January 2012, Victorino Chua was arrested at his home in Stockport. His neighbours were stunned. They all reported that he was a gentle, caring man. There was nothing about him to suggest he was a mass-murderer.

A few days after he was arrested, he was released on bail, but not allowed to return to the hospital. He did interviews with the media in an attempt to clear his name, though it was noted that he never once said that he didn't kill the patients. Instead he dwelt on his own struggle with injustice and suicidal thoughts.

It was not until March he was charged with the murders of Tracy Arden, Alfred Weaver and Arnold Lancaster. He was also charged with 31 other offences, including causing grievous bodily harm and attempted poisoning. The court proceedings lasted three months, and at no point did Chua's motive ever become clear. The only hint came from a letter he'd written but never sent that the police had found while searching his home. In it, he admitted that he had deceived his friends and colleagues, saying: 'They thought I'm a nice person but there a devil in me.' He told the police that he had written it to a girlfriend who he had had an extramarital affair with.

Chua tried to blame burnout, saying that he was working 66 hours a week. But there was evidence suggesting he was fully aware of his actions when he committed them. When he took a blood sample from 41-year-old Grant Misell, one of the 22 patients who had been poisoned, he recorded that Misell was responsive and alert. At the time, he was deep in a hypoglycemic coma and was left with brain damage.

After a three-month trial, Victorino Chua was found guilty of murdering Tracy Arden and Alfred Weaver. He was cleared of murdering Arnold Lancaster as it was found that Lancaster had actually succumbed to cancer. However, Chua was still convicted of attempting to cause him grievous bodily harm by poisoning, along with a string of other offences. He showed no emotion when he was given 25 life sentences. He won't be eligible for parole until 2049.

NIELS HÖGEL

onvicted of killing 85 and claiming to have killed over 300, Niels Högel is considered the most prolific serial killer in the history of peacetime Germany – perhaps in the world. Despite the death toll, it took colleagues over four years to spot what he was up to and report it to the police. And the authorities took more than a decade to conduct a full investigation.

'If it is possible that in Germany more than 300 deaths over 15 years can be swept under the carpet, what else is possible?' said Christian Marbach, whose grandfather was a victim. 'What does it take for people in Germany to stand up and pay attention?'

Frank Lauxtermann, the only former colleague who testified openly about working alongside Högel, said: 'A culture of looking away and keeping your head down ultimately shielded the suspect.'

Born in 1976 in Wilhelmshaven, Högel followed his father and grandmother into nursing. His mother was a paralegal and he also lived with an older sister. There was nothing unusual about his upbringing which he described a sheltered and protected. After completing his vocational training in 1997 at the Sankt-Willehad-Hospital in Wilhelmshaven, Högel became a nurse and continued working there. By the time he married in 2004 and his daughter was born, he was well into his career as a murderer.

In 1999, Högel moved to the Oldenberg Clinic in a city 48 km (30 miles) to the south. There he worked in Ward 211, the intensive care unit for patients who had undergone cardiac surgery. In August 2001, he attended a meeting when doctors and medical orderlies discussed the spike in deaths and emergency resuscitations that had occurred in the previous few months. Fifty-eight per cent of these had happened while Högel was on duty.

Indeed, he was know as the 'Resuscitation Rambo' because of the way he pushed everyone else aside when a patient needed resuscitating. His colleagues rewarded his skill with a necklace made of injection tubes, which he wore with pride. They did not know that, in many cases, he had caused the problem in the first place so that he could bask in their plaudits.

After the meeting, Högel called in sick for three weeks, fearing he had been found out. During that time only two patients died, a rate far lower than when he had been on call. Under pressure from the head of Ward 211, Högel was transferred to the anaesthesiology ward, but the head physician there too became suspicious that Högel was nearly always present when emergencies occurred.

Glowing reference

The matter was referred to the head of the clinic who called Högel in to discuss the number of patients under his care who had lapsed into life-threatening conditions for no obvious reasons. He was given a choice. Either he transfer to the clinic's logistics unit – that is, become a glorified hospital porter – or quit with three-months' severance pay. He chose the latter, leaving with a glowing letter of reference that described him as someone who worked 'independently and conscientiously'. In a crisis, it said, he reacted 'with consideration' and was 'technically correct'.

There was no hint of the suspicions that his colleagues harboured, or that he had effectively been barred from contact with patients or encouraged to resign. Rather, he had a 'circumspect, diligent and autonomous' work ethic and had acted 'prudently and in an objectively correct manner in critical situations'. The director of nursing also praised his 'devotedness' and 'cooperative conduct'. The letter concluded with an overall assessment of Högel, saying he had completed tasks he was assigned to 'to the utmost satisfaction'.

This faultless reference secured him a job at the intensive care unit of the Delmenhorst hospital in the suburbs of Bremen some 32 km (20 miles) away. Highly regarded at first, before long, similar suspicions arose at Delmenhorst. Within four months, a patient, Brigitte A., died under his care. Others, Hans S., Christoph K. and Josef Z., followed. All were identified with only a last initial under German privacy laws. They had died from arrhythmia or a sudden drop in blood pressure while Högel was on duty.

Again colleagues had their suspicions. A colleague at Delmenhorst, identified only as Susanna K., testified: 'In the beginning, you just think it is fate. But at some point you grow distrustful.'

She said Högel's colleagues in Oldenburg had talked about him, but did not go to their superiors or lodge a complaint out of fear of being reprimanded or because they didn't see it as their business in a country where citizens closely guard their privacy. When another nurse in Delmenhorst told her superior she was suspicious of Högel, no action was taken and she never followed up.

The state prosecutor said that the nurse's colleagues in Delmenhorst had enough clues pointing to the gruesome motive behind his actions from at least 9 or 10 May 2005 that they would have been 'obligated to intervene'.

Four empty vials

It was not until 22 June 2005 that Renate T., a fellow nurse in Delmenhorst, took action after discovering Högel standing over a 63-year-old lung cancer patient, Dieter Maass. His life support system had been switched off, and in the trash lay four empty vials of gilurytmal or ajmaline – a drug that induces arrhythmia – though no doctor had prescribed the medication for him at the time. She quickly took a blood sample and sent it for tests. The next day Maass was dead.

When the test results showed a dangerously high dose of heart medication, the doctor and nurse in charge of the case met to discuss the situation. But they let Högel finish his shift. In those hours, 67-year-old Renate Röper became his final victim and the police were called in.

Other colleagues then voiced their suspicions that Högel was connected to numerous complications, resuscitations and unexplained deaths at their hospital.

The police began examining all deaths at the hospital between 2003 and 2005, finding they had doubled since Högel had come to work there. In 2005, nearly three-quarters of the deaths had occurred during or immediately after his shifts. Nevertheless, in December 2006, he was tried only for the death of Dieter Maass. Found guilty of voluntary manslaughter, he was sentenced to five years in prison and banned from nursing for the same period. On appeal, the sentence was upped to seven-and-a-half years in prison and a life-long ban from nursing.

But that was not the end of the matter. In January 2014, the Oldenburg district attorney's office began further investigations into the incidents at the Delmenhorst Clinic. That September, Högel was charged with three new counts of murder and two counts of attempted murder. After confessing to the charges, Högel stated he had committed a further 30 murders. He had administered 90 unauthorized and potentially lethal injections, but 60 patients had been successfully revived.

At a second trial that ended in 2015 he was jailed for life for two murders and two attempted murders. The police went on to identify some 200 suspicious deaths connected to Högel and a special commission was set up to investigate. Some 134 bodies in 67 cemeteries in Germany, Poland and Turkey were exhumed and autopsied. Many revealed traces of heart medication. Some were so badly decayed that detection was impossible and over a hundred of the bodies of those who had died in Delmenhorst had been cremated.

By November 2016, the authorities said they could prove that Högel had killed 37 in Delmenhorst between December 2002 and June 2005. By August 2017, that number had risen to 90. By November, 107, and he was charged with a further 100 homicides – 36 in Oldenburg and 64 in Delmenhorst.

In June 2019, 42-year-old Niels Högels was found guilty of the murder of 85 patients in his care, some as young as 34, others as old as 96. It was found that he had systematically injected patients with cardiovascular medication in order to trigger a medical emergency and show off his resuscitation skills. He was cleared of only 14 counts, but confessed to 43 murders. In 52 instances, he said he simply could not remember.

This time Högel, who had sat through previous trials silent and sullen, testified in court. Often, he recalled remarkable details surrounding the deaths. In other cases, he offered the same mechanical answer: 'I have no memory, but I can't rule out a manipulation.'

He also told the court that he felt 'shame' when reading the medical records of the patients he was thought to have killed.

'Every single case, even just reading them,' he said, 'I am endlessly sorry.'

In the last hearing before sentencing, Högel had asked the relatives of his victims for forgiveness. 'I want to apologize wholeheartedly to every single one of you for what I have done over the years,' he said. Over the course of the trial, he said he had come to realize the amount of suffering his 'terrible deeds' had caused.

But many observers questioned the sincerity of Högel's apology. Until eventually confessing to some of the killings, he had sworn on his daughter's life that he had not killed anyone. One expert witness described Högel as a 'competent liar'.

Gaby Lübben, one of the lawyers representing victims' relatives, told the newspaper *Bild* that Högel's apology was not credible: 'He only acted out his remorse to gather plus points... He should have stayed silent.'

Dr Karl-Heinz Beine, a leading German neurologist and head of psychiatry at St Marien Hospital in Hamm said Högel appeared to be driven by narcissism and a need to fill a deep lack of self-worth.

Another psychiatrist expert witness said during the trial that while the accused nurse had displayed traits of noticeable personality disorders, such as a lack of shame, guilt and empathy, these were not so severe as to nullify responsibility.

'I personally am convinced that the defendant continues to live out his narcissism today,' said Arne Schmidt, the police chief who led the special investigation into the killings for the Oldenburg police from 2014 to 2017. 'Only when presented with enough evidence would Mr Högel confess. The nurse had revelled in playing God.'

There is no death penalty in Germany. Judge Sebastian Buehrmann gave Högel another life sentence, saying his killing spree was incomprehensible. Taking prior convictions into account, he declared Högel's 'severe gravity of guilt', a German legal term which significantly increases the respective sentence's severity and precludes a chance of early release which was usually allowed after the prisoner had served 15 years.

'The purpose of this trial is to provide answers for the family members whose loved ones died, to help them to understand how and why,' Judge Bührmann had said. However, he regretted that the court had not been able to 'lift the fog' for many grieving relatives. Some said they struggled with the uncertainty of not knowing if their loved one was murdered or not.

'It's very, very tough,' said Frank Brinkers, who had lost his father.

'I went through hell,' Brinkers told the German news agency DPA, adding that he had hoped his father's case would turn out to be unequivocal. 'It appears that wasn't meant to be.'

Mariya Tüter said she expected more. Three years earlier, the police told her they suspected that her husband, Adnan, might have been murdered by Högel. Since then, she had struggled with depression and, at times, it was so severe that she could not even to drive to the supermarket.

'Until this happened, I saw doctors as people who did the right thing; they were there to be trusted,' she said. 'But in this case, they swept everything under the carpet. I finally want justice to be served.'

Four of Högel's former colleagues at the Delmenhorst clinic, including two senior doctors, the head of the intensive care unit and one of his deputies, were accused of manslaughter. Others in the administration of the two hospitals were accused of having turned a blind eye to unusually high mortality rates.

'Niels Högel is a member of this extreme minority,' said Dr Beine, who has researched serial killers in the medical profession since 1989. He said that what struck him about Mr Högel's testimony was his lack of empathy, even when speaking to victims' families.

ELIZABETH WETTLAUFER

Registered nurse Elizabeth Wettlaufer pleaded guilty to eight counts of first degree murder, four counts of attempted murder and two counts of aggravated assault. Worryingly, her crimes may never have been discovered if she had not gone to great lengths to have her confessions taken seriously. She had to check into a mental health clinic to make sure that her confessions were not just heard, but heeded. She had already told a former boyfriend, an ex-girlfriend, a nursing colleague, a lawyer and a pastor and his wife that she was a killer. None of them reported her to the police.

When she told a Narcotics Anonymous adviser they dismissed her as a 'pathological liar'. The ex-boyfriend attributed her admission of killing nursing home patients in her care to a 'psychiatric episode'. The pastor prayed over her and told her not to kill again, otherwise he would turn her in.

Wettlaufer was born Elizabeth Mae Parker in Woodstock, Ontario, on 10 June 1967 to strict Baptist parents. As a child, Beth was shy, awkward and a target of bullying. Other kids called her 'little Bethie Parker', which she hated. To counter this she added an e to Beth, calling herself Bethe in an effort to appear special. It did no good.

Her controlling father Doug and other elders at his fundamentalist church appear to have been homophobic and deeply disapproved of her association with childhood friend Glen Hart, who was homosexual. At school she developed homosexual tendencies of her own, but was rebuffed by another girl.

She was goalkeeper in the hockey team and was in the school band. But there was another side to her. She once set off the fire alarm in the hope that a boy she didn't like would get into trouble.

She also wrote poetry and studied journalism in college, but dropped out after a year. Instead she studied religious education counselling at London Baptist Bible College. Her father took courses at the college to keep a close eye on her and she was once sent home after she visited a gay-friendly church with a girlfriend.

Conversion therapy

Attempts were made with 'conversion therapy' to 'un-gay' her. This resulted in a loss of confidence and self-loathing. Nevertheless, in 1997, she married Donnie Wettlaufer, a long-distance truck driver she met at church. They lived together in a bungalow in Woodstock, but did not have any children.

By then she had studied nursing at Conestoga College in Kitchener, Ontario, becoming a registered nurse in 1995. Meanwhile she did various jobs around Woodstock, including working for a social services agency caring for disabled people. She began displaying the symptoms of bipolar disorder and began abusing alcohol and opioids, later claiming she had sought treatment for her mental condition. After an overdose, she was temporarily unable to work, but picked up the odd shift as a personal support worker in various care homes.

Seeking help from other women online led her husband to suspect she was having an affair. They split up and eventually divorced with him dismissing her as 'sick'. She did indeed enter into a long-term relationship with another women. They moved in together and got engaged after same-sex marriage was legalized in Ontario in 2003.

In 2007, Wettlaufer found a fulltime job in a nursing home called Caressant Care in Woodstock, the largest in the region. Paying $60,000 a year, it gave her the financial stability she needed. The new job also came with a significant amount of responsibility. Working mostly at night, Wettlaufer was in charge of 32 elderly patients, their medication and upkeep.

Initially thought to be professional and caring, her behaviour began to deteriorate. 'You have an extensive disciplinary record for medication-related errors which includes numerous warnings as well as one, three, and two five day suspensions,' one report said.

She was accused of turning up to work drunk. Once on a night shift, she was found passed out in the basement. She got her nursing licence restricted after she was caught stealing medication for pain relief and suffered a near-fatal overdose.

By then she had 12 years' experience in nursing. Her elderly patients often had blood-sugar problems and she would inject insulin when necessary. She did this at her own discretion and Caressant Care did not keep a close eye on its stocks of insulin. The procedure was straightforward. Cartridges of insulin were inserted into an insulin 'pen'. At one end was a needle, at the other a dial which regulated the dose.

It took Wettlaufer a little time to work out how much insulin it would take to kill a patient. She would turn the dial up, then stick the needle into some discreet spot on the victim's body. This would send their blood-sugar level crash diving, putting them into hypoglycemic shock.

Soon after she arrived at Caressant, Wettlaufer tried this out on 87-year-old dementia-sufferer Clotilde Adriano. She survived but only because other staff noticed she was failing and managed to restore her blood-sugar levels. Later, in her confession to the police, Wettlaufer said she hadn't really wanted Adriano to die.

'I just don't know. I was angry and, um, had this sense inside me that she might be a person God wanted back with him,' she said. 'I honestly felt that God wanted to use me.'

Adriano was the widowed mother of two and grandmother of five. She died the following year, but no blame reflected on Wettlaufer.

Next Wettlaufer continued her experiments with Adriano's sister-in-law, Albina Demedeiros, who was also in the care home, although she didn't kill her either. She died three years later. Again her death was not attributed to Wettlaufer.

After three months at Caressant Care, Wettlaufer actually managed to kill a patient. This was 84-year-old James Silcox, a World War II veteran who had been immobilized by a stroke. On 11 August 2007, Wettlaufer had started a double shift and found Silcox agitated, unsure of where he was and calling out for his wife Agnes. Wefflaufer said she felt a 'red surge'. She was angry with Silcox and admitted that she wanted him to die.

At around 9.30 p.m., she went to the medical storage room and loaded an insulin pen with 50 units of quick-acting insulin. This was twice as much as she had use on Adriano and Demedeiros. Before he lost consciousness, Silcox called out: 'I'm sorry. I love you.' It's not clear who he was addressing. Wettlaufer claimed to feel pangs of guilt about what she had done, but also said it felt 'like a pressure had been relieved from me'.

It wasn't until 22 December that she killed again – this time 84-year-old mechanic and father of two Maurice 'Moe' Granat. Death could be painless and relatively quick, over in a few hours. But sometimes, the victim's body would contort and they would foam at the mouth. In some cases, the victim would slip into an irreversible vegetative state for days before finally dying.

On 1 January 2008, Wettlaufer injected 63-year-old father-of-two Michael Priddle with insulin 'with intent to murder'. He survived and died at home the following year with his wife of 41 years by his side. The police did not attribute his death to Wettlaufer.

According to court documents, Wettlaufer was deranged, but never incapable of distinguishing right from wrong. She exhibited 'significant symptoms of borderline personality disorder' – notably mood instability, impulsivity, fear of abandonment, unstable relationships and anger. As well as suffering from mental illness, she was also dependent on drugs, though she had been able to function while using them for many years.

'Much of this behaviour seemed to have worsened since her husband left, but this behaviour was present prior to her marriage as well,' one medical report said, but concluded that from the age of 15 she had developed an 'antisocial personality disorder'. She also had 'difficulties with being brought up in a controlled Baptist home environment'. Wettlaufer struggled with her religious beliefs. She was a regular and committed church-goer, but a conflicted one.

After her divorce she seemed less conflicted about her sexual identity and would often go surfing for lesbian love online. By early 2008, Wettlaufer's relationship with her fiancée had ended, and she had connected with Sheila Andrews, a prison cafeteria worker in Prince Albert, Saskatchewan. That summer, Andrews invited her to come to stay for a week. It was a mistake.

When Wettlaufer got off the plane, she immediately demanded hugs and kisses, telling Andrews that she had told everyone at her work how much she loved her and they were going to get together. Andrews said she thought it would be better to get to know each other first.

They spent the first night together at a motel near the airport. The next morning Andrews was already convinced that the relationship with Wettlaufer was not going to work out.

'She pouted a lot and [had] little temper tantrums, you know, like if she didn't get something her own way, like my affection and stuff like that,' said Andrews. 'There was a lot of childish issues with her, and I just thought, "You're a grown woman. Act like it."'

Despite her training, Wettlaufer showed no interest in meeting Andrew's ailing mother. However, she was proud of being a nurse.

'I think she liked the fact that she was in charge in the evenings,' said Andrews. 'She enjoyed the power. I think she enjoyed that the most.'

When Wettlaufer returned to work, the relationship was over, leaving her dejected and bitter. She began posting self-pitying verses on a poetry website. On 1 September 2008, she injected 57-year-old Wayne Hedges with insulin – again 'with intent to kill'.

On 13 October 2011, Wettlaufer killed 87-year-old widowed mother-of-two Gladys Millard with insulin at the Caressant Care home. Twelve days later she murdered 95-year-old Helen Matheson, also a widowed mother of two. Then on 6 November, she used insulin to murder 96-year-old Mary Zurawinski. Nothing suspicious was reported and there were no post mortems as, at Caressant, it was up to Wettlaufer to alert authorities if a suspicious death occurred on her shift.

By this time, Wettlaufer was heavily addicted to hydromorphone. She kept closer tabs on Caressant's hydromorphone stocks than on insulin. She also stole drugs from patients.

'Some had... confusion, so they couldn't tell the difference between what pills you were giving them. I could give them a laxative instead of their hydromorphone,' she told the police. Sometimes she would open the capsule, swallow the contents and give the patient an empty pill case. Or else she would take the pills of patients who had already died.

The intake of hydromorphone kept Wettlaufer calm and she did not kill again for two years. But in 2013, she found 90-old Helen Young 'very difficult to deal with'. On 13 July, she gave her two massive injections of insulin. Over the next three hours, Young's face went red, her eyes bulged and her limbs bent inward, the result of a seizure induced by the insulin overdoses. By morning, she was dead, leaving Wettlaufer to comfort her weeping niece. Describing the crime to police, Wettlaufer said she felt 'the surging' again. Afterwards there was 'laughter', which was like 'a cackling from the pit of hell'.

Deadly secrets

Sometimes she felt pangs of guilt. At the time, Wettlaufer was attending the multi-denominational Family Church in Woodstock. That summer, she said she drove to her pastor's home and revealed her deadly secrets to him and his wife.

'They prayed over me,' Wettlaufer told police. 'And they said to me how this was God's grace. "But if you ever do this again, we will have to turn you in to the police."' The pastor told police he wasn't sure whether to believe what Wettlaufer had told him.

Though none of her colleagues suspected that Wettlaufer was killing patients using insulin, she made other mix-ups with medication which harmed patients and she was fired. Within weeks she was hired by Meadow Park Long Term Care in London, Ontario. Within a month, she had murdered 75-year-old Arpad Horvath with insulin.

Soon after she quit and went into rehab for a month. Two months after that she was working part-time at Telfer Place retirement home in Paris, Ontario, where she injected 77-year-old dementia-sufferer Sandra Towler with insulin 'with intent to murder'. Towler slipped into hypoglycaemic shock. She was saved by other staff, who intervened just in time.

In the summer of 2016, Wettlaufer wrote to her old flame Sheila Andrews through Facebook Messenger, saying: 'I am restless tonight. Hyper about my job. Having a hard time getting one of the required skills right. The skill is changing the dressing on an IV line that goes directly to the heart. I violated the sterile field and put things in the wrong place today.'

The case Wettlaufer was referring to was that of Bev Bertram, a 68-year-old woman she was caring for in Ingersoll, Ontario. Bertram lived a sheltered life with her partner in a public housing complex.

Police would later accuse Wettlaufer of stealing insulin from another patient and administering a lethal dose of it into a catheter in Bertram's arm 'with intent to murder'. Again the intended victim survived.

At the time, Wettlaufer was working with a nursing agency which gave her a placement at a school programme in Ingersoll that needed help treating children with diabetes. Again she would be administering insulin. Who better for the job? Unable to trust herself, Wettlaufer refused and quit nursing entirely. Realizing that she needed psychiatric help, she took a train to Toronto and checked herself into the emergency ward at the Centre for Addiction and Mental Health (CAMH). Over the next 20 days, she confessed to anyone who would listen.

Her psychiatrist Dr Alan Kahn suggested they she commit her confession to paper, though warning her that anything she revealed would be handed over to the police. She produced a four-page handwritten confession. The police picked her up from CAMH and she gave a recorded statement at the local police station. The Ontario police were then informed and a massive murder investigation ensued.

Three days after being discharged from CAMH she was arrested. She pleaded guilty to all charges and was sentenced to eight consecutive life sentences with no possibility of parole for 25 years. She also lost her nursing licence. Later she was transferred to a medical facility for treatment.

PICTURE CREDITS

Alamy: 79
APA: 149
Barrington Barber: 9
Corbis: 25, 112, 181, 205
Fairfax Media: 199
Getty Images: 125, 132, 192
Peter Gray: 209
Press Association: 97, 155, 166
Shutterstock Editorial: 74
Topfoto: 45, 173
Wikimedia Commons: 88, 92